MW00792091

Multiplying the Witness

Dedicated to
Luther Wesley Smith
a Christian minister with vision and faith
whose enthusiastic and discerning leadership
gave the
American Baptist Churches in the U.S.A.
years of extraordinary achievement
in educational ministries

Multiplying the Witness

150 Years of American Baptist Educational Ministries

LAWRENCE T. SLAGHT

Judson Press, Valley Forge

MULTIPLYING THE WITNESS

Copyright © 1974
Judson Press, Valley Forge, PA 19481

Library of Congress Cataloging in Publication Data

Slaght, Lawrence T.
   Multiplying the witness.

     1. American Baptist Churches in the U.S.A.
Board of Educational Ministries.
2. Baptists—Education. 3. Baptists—Publishing. I. Title.
Z473.A47S55   070.5'73   73-16789
ISBN 0-8170-0634-6

Printed in the U.S.A.

Foreword

The story began one hundred fifty years ago. It is impressive. It includes the colporter plodding through the wilderness with books in baskets balanced across his shoulders.

It also includes educational executives streaking through the jet streams of the nation. More impressive than the difference is the common commitment—that of sharing a WORD.

Dr. Lawrence T. Slaght brings care and competence to the historical task. His technical training is that of a church historian. His wealth of experience includes pastoral responsibility in both the East and West. He has also served as a theological professor and a religious editor.

Forty years ago Lawrence Slaght entered an American Baptist college as a student. He has been related to institutions served by the American Baptist Board of Educational Ministries every year since that time. He is supportive of and concerned for this work. He is also knowledgeable of its weaknesses and critical of its shortcomings. Hence this book is no public relations thing. Your reading of this volume will be a rubbing of mind with a man of insight and integrity.

American Baptist Educational Ministries is the story of *mission*. It is well known that the modern missionary movement was initiated by

Adoniram Judson of Burma. The story also includes the second missionary, George Hough, who was the forerunner of American Baptist Educational Ministries. Hough was a printer who responded to Judson's earnest plea to bring the light of the written Word to Southeast Asia.

The base of this "multiplying witness" was the Baptist General Tract Society, founded one hundred fifty years ago. It was a response to Judson's cry for needed tracts. It was also a meeting of John Mason Peck's demand for Christian literature on the American frontier. The mission was carried on horseback to obscure settlements, distant villages, and lonely farm people. Sunday school missionaries traversed the continent. Chapel cars carried the Word by rail. And the mission continues.

This is also the story of *expansion*. It was a long step from that first year when less than $375 was spent in publishing nineteen tracts to the present annual budget of almost $8,000,000. It was sacrifice and stewardship which expanded that original legacy of $20 to the present investment portfolio of approximately $9,000,000. Dozens of colleges, thousands of professors, and multitudes of students have profited from this educational ministry of American Baptists. Four modern bookstores now service the nation. Dozens of new books issue each year from a modern printing plant in historic Valley Forge.

This is also a story of *relevance*. The expertise of theological scholars and biblical specialists is carefully graded to the needs of every age level. Three hundred campuses are fields of mission. Hundreds of theological students are preparing to proclaim the gospel in an idiom communicable to people of the space age.

Nor are those outside the mainstream forgotten. Christian literature is published in Braille. Bibles are printed in Russian for use both in the United States and behind the iron curtain. The devotional booklet, *Secret Place*, is provided free to hospitals and prisons.

It's a great story. It includes a dauntless John Mason Peck as corresponding secretary and a dynamic Luther Wesley Smith as the chief executive. It includes the generous James L. Kraft and the anonymous child in a rural church.

It even includes you!

ROBERT C. CAMPBELL
General Secretary
American Baptist Churches in the U.S.A.

Preface

To give an account of the legacy which Baptists have received from their forefathers in the form known as the Board of Educational Ministries is an awesome task. The passage of 150 years in an endeavor as wide sweeping as the Christian education of a whole denomination through church and school; through authorship and publication; through the academe of college, seminary, and assembly can only have occurred because a host of people took their responsibility seriously. We have tried to tell the story of some, for how can we know where we are going if we do not know where we have been?

Such an accounting, of necessity, must leave unmentioned the names and deeds of most. We rest in the assurance that these are "known unto God." However, the author cannot escape his indebtedness to those who made this volume possible—first, to the Sesquicentennial Committee, who gave him the assignment and who supported him with their confidence: Elbert E. Gates, Jr., chairman; Samuel S. Deibler, Jr.; Weimer K. Hicks; Grady W. Powell; and Jo Ann Smith; to members of the B.E.M. staff: Lester C. Garner, who gave administrative leadership; Madelene Andrews, who supplied invaluable data; and Dorothy Martin, who made the library files available; to Edward Starr of the American Baptist Historical Society; to editors Frank Hoadley and Harold Twiss for their most substantial efforts; to the divisional directors for their guidance, Peter Jensh of Publishing and Business; Grant Hanson of Church Education; and Robert Davis of Christian Higher Education; to Harold Richardson, under whose administration the project began, and to William McKee, under whose administration the matter was brought to completion; and finally, and most importantly, to Irene Swanson Slaght, wife, counselor, typist, researcher, and confidante. To these, and to the many others who helped along the way, we are deeply grateful.

LAWRENCE T. SLAGHT

Contents

   (Earlier Board members are listed in *The First Hundred Years of the American Baptist Publication Society* and *Pioneers of Light,* both published in 1924 for the Centennial.)

1. Establishing the Witnes

The Creation of the Baptist General Tract Society

One does not usually associate college newspapers with a call to proclaim "The Everlasting Gospel," but that was precisely the masthead banner of *The Star,* a publication of Columbian College, Washington, D.C., in the 1820s. The issue for February 14, 1824, for instance, had for its lead editorial a two-column argument on "Prayer for Children." The editor was for it. He did not think it would lead to infant sprinkling! He also found it newsworthy to report the deaths in the city of Washington the previous month. There were thirty. Twelve of those died of measles, two of whom were "coloured." The proceedings of Congress were reported. Items included were: an appropriations bill for the navy, a bill "to abolish imprisonment for debt," a measure to disseminate smallpox vaccine, a measure to authorize subscriptions for the Chesapeake and Delaware Canal, and another for a road "from Wheeling in the State of Virginia, to the Seat of Government in Missouri." The page also carried an ad for Daniel Webster's speech on the "Greek Revolution." Copies could be purchased for 12½ cents each.

Amidst this potpourri of the sacred and secular was a brief item which was to validate the paper's masthead and to have an even more far-reaching effect than the banishing of smallpox or the building of a national highway to the West. It was a letter to the editor suggesting the formation of a Tract Society for Baptists. The editor had published it to see what would happen.

ORGANIZING FOR ACTION

What happened was that a number of readers acted promptly on the proposal and arranged a meeting for Wednesday, February 25, to implement the plan. Out of this came the organization of the Baptist General Tract Society. Over the years this became known in succession as the American Baptist Publication and Sunday School Society, the American Baptist Publication Society, the American Baptist Board of Education and Publication, and most recently the Board of Educational Ministries of the American Baptist Churches in the U.S.A.

The objective of the Society was established at the first meeting— "to disseminate evangelical truth, and to inculcate sound morals" through educational means. As times changed, the approach, the emphasis, the technique may have changed, but the basic task has remained constant. The assigned and accepted commission has been that of *multiplying the witness* through the distribution of printed material and through the proclamation and interpretation of the gospel by qualified educational specialists. As the first 150 years of service come to a close, three-quarters of a million people, young and old, are enrolled in church schools which depend in whole or in part on materials and services supplied by the Board of Educational Ministries, and thirty thousand students are registered in institutions of higher learning related to the Board. With a modern printing plant producing and shipping between four and five million pounds of materials per year and with a budget of over seven million dollars, the Board of Educational Ministries is truly fulfilling the commission. The witness *is* being multiplied, sound morals *are* being taught, and the word *is* being distributed.

THE NEED FOR ACTION

The need for a means to implement the educational ministries of concerned Baptists was manifest even in those early days. The nation had established its independence in 1776, its Constitution in 1789, and its sovereign power with the War of 1812. It had assumed the position of defender of the independence of the Western Hemisphere by the Monroe Doctrine of 1823, and by 1824 it was well on its way with a westward movement that would not only cross the Allegheny Mountains but would also claim the mighty Mississippi Valley and even the mountains and deserts of the far West to the Pacific Coast. A great nation was developing, and discipleship-minded Baptists certainly could not ignore this opened door.

Something less than three million people lived in these United States at the time of the break with the English throne. By 1825 the population had risen to over ten million. Baptist growth had followed, even led, the national pattern. From a small, neglected, and ignored group at the beginning of the struggle for liberty their numbers had increased so that by the time the Tract Society was formed in 1824 there were more than 200,000 Baptists in the country, mostly along the Atlantic coast from Maine to Georgia and westward through the Blue Ridge Mountains as far as Kentucky and Tennessee. Certainly a group of this size was an adequate foundation upon which to build. The demands which some 3,500 churches and an unknown number of Sunday schools, Bible classes, and other groups could place upon a religious publishing house can only be imagined. Thousands had been won to Christ, many in times of recent religious fervor. They needed instruction. Millions more lived outside the household of God. They needed conversion. For this two-fold task the printing press proved to be a magnificent helper.

Although Baptists were more interested in soul liberty than in systematization, they realized that some arrangement for association was necessary. They recognized that totally independent congregations quickly became vulnerable to attack from both without and within, and that some degree of mutuality must be established. Thus, associations of churches were developed, to be followed by state conventions. Indeed, during the decade of the 1820s—the time of the founding of the Tract Society—state associations or conventions were established in Maine, Vermont, New Hampshire, Massachusetts, Rhode Island, Connecticut, New York, New Jersey, Pennsylvania, Virginia, North Carolina, South Carolina, Georgia, and Alabama. Even more prominent, of course, was the formation of a national body for the support of Adoniram Judson and others in the enterprise of foreign missions, not quite ten years before the Tract Society came into being.

THE FOUNDERS

Who were those twenty-five men who met at 923 E Street, NW,

Washington, D.C., on that memorable occasion 150 years ago? And who were those who rallied to their cause?

George Wood. The host of the meeting was George Wood. Next door to Mr. Wood, i.e., at 925 E Street, *The Columbian Star* was printed. This paper had sounded the first call to action and on that printing press some of the first publications were prepared. George Wood was greatly responsible for these contributions. In spite of ill health occasioned by too close confinement in office work, he became the first agent of the Society. He was also among the first to perceive that the best interests of the new organization would best be served by moving it from the largely undeveloped capital city to Philadelphia, where facilities were far superior.

Luther Rice. Much better known than George Wood to Baptists, then and now, was Luther Rice, the first treasurer of the Society. Among the prime movers of the Baptist enterprise in the early part of the nineteenth century it would be difficult to find anyone more involved than he. Rice had been born in Northborough, Massachusetts, educated at Williams College, prepared for the ministry at Andover Seminary, and had been president of the student Society of Inquiry on the Subject of Missions, from which came missionaries Judson and Newell. Rice had been promised that he, too, could be appointed a missionary if he would raise his own expenses, a matter which he accomplished promptly. By August, 1812, he had arrived in India. Thus, by the age of twenty-nine he had completed formal professional training, helped organize the American Board of Commissioners for Foreign Missions (Congregational), been ordained a minister, been appointed a missionary, and actually arrived on the field!

Convinced, by his study of the Bible, that immersion was the only proper method of baptism, Rice was baptized on confession of faith November 1, 1812. Seven weeks earlier, Judson had come to the same conclusion and had also been immersed. Perplexed as to the next proper step and harassed by the English authorities in India, Rice proposed to return to the United States to explain matters to the Congregationalists and, in the event of failure there, to arouse Baptist interest and support from them for missions. Judson, for his part, would go on to Burma. So these two great giants of the church took their separate, but complementary, ways to glorious service.

On arriving back in Boston, Rice was not happily received by the disenchanted Congregationalists; so he turned to the Baptists. His newfound friends welcomed him with open arms, open minds, and open pocketbooks. Appointed agent for a newly organized group of Baptists, Luther Rice was commissioned to go up and down the land enlisting financial support for the cause of missions. Less than a year later, in May, 1814, a substantial group assembled at Philadelphia and organized the General Missionary Convention of the Baptist Denomination in the United States for Foreign Missions—a direct ancestor of the American Baptist Foreign Mission Society.

Not content with these labors, Rice added the cause of Christian higher education to his already full portfolio of mission interests. He urged the establishment of Columbian College (now George Washington University) in Washington, D.C. He led in the purchase of the campus, helped Dr. Staughton move from his Philadelphia pastorate to the college presidency, got the newly organized convention to take the college under its supervision, became agent for and treasurer of the college, and founded *The Columbian Star* as a Baptist weekly newspaper. At the same time, the busy Rice was raising funds for his missionary companions in Burma!

Noah Davis. Another attendant at the organizational meeting of the Tract Society (and indeed its spark of inspiration) was Noah Davis, of the Baptist Church at Salisbury, Maryland, and a dropout from Columbian College. He was, however, not a dropout from Christianity. In fact he was the author of the momentous letter to the editor of *The Columbian Star* on February 14, 1824, that had ignited the fire of interest for Christian publications. His letter had drawn attention to the fact that the Congregationalists were multiplying the witness by the distribution of tracts. He saw printed media as ideal for taking the gospel to America's vast interior where there were simply not enough ministers and missionaries to make all the contacts.

Noah Davis was one of those rare individuals who easily blended vision with action. Unwilling to delay his active ministry until the completion of his college course, he had left school midway and begun a full-time ministry. He had first labored among the churches on the lower Delmarva Peninsula where the antimissionary spirit was so disastrously effective that in Delaware not one of the early Baptist churches would survive. Then he had moved across the bay to Norfolk, Virginia, and turned his attention to a ministry among the sailors. He had formed a benefit society on their behalf and compiled a hymnbook for their use.

Although the founders of the Tract Society initially overlooked the

Noah Davis

creative and energetic Noah Davis and instead appointed George Wood as their first agent, Mr. Wood's resignation at the close of the second year reopened the position. Noah Davis, called by Wood "a Mr. Greatheart," now volunteered to take his place, and his offer was soon accepted. Perhaps a bit more prudence on the part of Mr. Davis in the expenditure of energy would have prolonged his own life, for he died July 15, 1830, after only three and one-half years of work as agent and business manager for the Society. But those were great and formative years, including among other developments the removal to Philadelphia which Davis insisted upon and which he managed with courage against bitter opposition.

William Staughton. Noah Davis's spiritual mentor was another mover in the birth and development of the Society—William Staughton. Born in England, Staughton had graduated from Bristol College in 1792, the year in which William Carey led in organizing the English Baptist Missionary Society at Kettering. Young Staughton had been one of that organizing group of twelve valiant spirits along with John Ryland and Andrew Fuller. The young preacher, strangely enough, did not feel called to remain in his homeland, although some splendid opportunities were open to him. There seemed to be no directive to accompany Carey to India, either. Instead, William Staughton sailed for America, where he became headmaster of an academy at Bordentown, New Jersey, and later established a school and a church at Burlington, New Jersey. Twelve years later (1805), he moved across the river and assumed the pulpit of the historic First Baptist Church of Philadelphia. He remained for eighteen years, active not only in the preaching of the gospel, a task at which he was a master (Princeton bestowed the Doctor of Divinity degree on him when he was only twenty-eight), but also in the development of other fields of service. In 1811 he organized from First Church a mission, to which the following year he was called as pastor. This became known as Fifth or Sansom Street Church. During his Philadelphia years he started in his home an informal theological seminary which he took to Washington with him and merged with the newly formed Columbian College when he was called to be its president in 1821. The theological department of Columbian was later removed to Newton Centre, Massachusetts, where it became Newton Theological Institution (now Andover Newton). Staughton was the first corresponding secretary of the American Baptist Foreign Mission Society and the father of the Philadelphia Bible Society. He was on his way to become president of Georgetown College, Kentucky, when he was taken ill and died.

John S. Meehan. Another Philadelphian and a Sunday school teacher in Dr. Staughton's church was also one of the founders of the Tract Society. This was John S. Meehan, a printer who had already set two tracts in type ready to be published whenever some group of Baptists would organize themselves for the work. Meehan moved his printing business to Washington at about the same time as Staughton's call to the presidency of Columbian College. Later he was to serve thirty-one years as librarian of Congress.

James Knowles. Another spiritual son of Dr. Staughton who was active in the formation of the society was James Knowles, a native of Providence, Rhode Island. Apprenticed at an early age to a printer, he was editor of a well-known paper by the time he was twenty-one. With a full and prosperous career opening before him, a radical Christian conversion experience turned him about and he entered the ministry. For preparation, he moved to Philadelphia and entered Dr. Staughton's school there, then went on to Washington with his mentor.

Among Knowles' schoolmates in Washington was Noah Davis, and between the two young men, earnest and eager for the gospel, there quickly developed a fast friendship. It was not long before Knowles became editor of *The Columbian Star,* and it was in this capacity that he received and published the letter of young Davis with strong editorial backing.

His, however, was not to be a career in religious journalism alone. A year after the founding of the Tract Society, he assumed the pastorate of the Second Baptist Church of Boston and later he

19

became professor at Newton Theological Institution. His first love never really departed, nonetheless, for he wrote a biography of Ann Hasseltine Judson and one of Roger Williams. In addition, he edited the seminary's *Christian Review* quarterly with distinction.

Samuel Cornelius. One more spiritual son of William Staughton who must be especially noted is Samuel Cornelius. A member of the great pastor's church in Philadelphia and a trainee for the ministry under Staughton, Cornelius followed the famous Dr. Spencer Cone as pastor of the Baptist Church in Alexandria, Virginia. It was in this place that he began the practice of carrying tracts in his top hat and distributing them as opportunity arose. Noticing this custom, Noah Davis seized upon it and gave the idea wings through his letter to the editor of *The Columbian Star* calling for the organization of a tract society for Baptists.

Samuel Cornelius was elected vice-president of the newly organized society in 1825, but did not remain in official capacity for long. Other interests drew him away—first Columbian College, then a pastorate in Mount Holly, New Jersey, and finally missionary work in Michigan.

Other Participants. Now what should be said of the others who were active in the founding of the Tract Society? Of Obadiah Brown, pastor of the First Baptist Church in Washington, a chaplain of Congress, and the first president of the society? Of Baron Stow, famed Boston preacher, elected a director at the age of twenty-five? Of Samuel Lynd, son-in-law to Dr. Staughton? Of Samuel Wait, a native of New York, a student at Columbian College, first secretary of the North Carolina Baptist Convention and president of Wake Forest College? Of Alexis Caswell, born in Taunton, Massachusetts, student, professor, president, trustee, and fellow of Brown University? Of Ira Chase, a son of Stratton, Vermont, a student of Dr. Staughton, and a longtime professor of biblical theology at Newton Theological Institution? Of John Bryce, pastor in Fredricksburg, Virginia, lawyer in Crawfordsville, Indiana, and mayor in Shreveport, Louisiana? And of Isaac Hutton, Joseph Gibson, Joseph Thaw, Enoch Reynolds, Reuben Johnson, Stephen Ustick, James Johnson, George Outlaw, and Daniel Cawood, about whom the record books are relatively silent? During the formative first year or two these all were present and accounted for as officers and directors of the new society organized to "multiply the witness" of Jesus Christ as Baptists understood it.

THE FIRST YEAR

The first year was a busy one, indeed, for the new organization. Simply stated the record shows that:

—19 tracts were printed.
—Total copies produced amounted to 85,000, of which 58,720 were distributed.
—10 depositories for the material were established.
—38 auxiliary societies were organized.
—25 local agents were engaged.

To support this effort, funds were required, and 150 years ago fund raising was more difficult even than today. According to the recording secretary's report of money received and entered into the treasury, cash came from near and far—from Washington, D.C., and from Norfolk, Richmond, and Union, Virginia; from Eatonton, Powellton, New Hope, and Harris's Neck, Georgia; from Cambridge and Zanesville, Ohio; from Jonesboro, Alabama; Fairfield, Vermont, and Salem, New Jersey. The "ladies of his congregation" contributed a life membership for Rev. Joseph Sheppard, of Salem, New Jersey. Similarly, did the women of Richard Furman's church in Charleston, South Carolina, honor their pastor. The ladies not only showed a womanly interest in matters ecclesiastical but were wise in their choices. Sheppard was the descendant of a long line of Baptist Sheppards in south Jersey, including David, who was a constituent of the historic Cohansie church in 1690, and Job, who was first pastor of the Salem church in 1755. Furman was the first president of the Triennial Convention. It was in recognition of his many talents that the Baptist university in South Carolina bears his name.

The sum given, $373.80, was not a great amount of money even in 1825, but it did represent a large measure of sacrifice. It was a solid step forward in Christian education and evangelism. It produced 696,000 pages of Christian witness.

Obviously the printing presses had been busy that first year, but what had they been producing? Here are titles of the first nineteen publications:

Constitution, Circular, etc.
Life of Bunyan
The Great Question Answered
Friendly Advice
The Pensioner

The Death Bed of a Medical Student
A Sunday's Excursion
The Two Apprentices
Thoughts on the Gospel
History of John Robbins, the Sailor
The Contrast
The Brazen Serpent
Address to the Sinner
Religion, the One Thing Needful
The Power of Conscience, or the Death of Altomont
Ellen, a Pleasing Instance of Early Piety
The Happy Waterman
The Way to Happiness
The Dreadful Superstition of the Hindoos

Several features are evident. The material was Baptist; the life of John Bunyan led the offerings. The material was evangelical: the "great question" was answered; the "brazen serpent" was lifted up; religion was "the one thing needful" for a joyous life in this world, but one should be prepared for the hereafter, remembering "the deathbed of a medical student," and surely the saints would care to speak an "address to the sinner." The material was positive and enthusiastic. The "waterman" was "happy" and the "way to happiness" could be delineated. However, not all things could be endorsed. "The dreadful superstition of the Hindoos" was a warning, but it was also a call to missionary activity.

RATIONALE

The underlying apologetic for this venture into the area of religious publications was well understood and argued by the founders of the Tract Society. Although Christians had established various Bible and missionary associations to strengthen their witness, there was no group specifically concerned with evangelistic literature. They saw the business of the Tract Society as the instrument to assail the hearts and engage the attention of the community. It was a part "of the moral machinery," as they reported in their first annual accounting. For the furtherance of Christ's work, they said, "The Bible and the preaching of the Gospel are undoubtedly the most desirable means." "But," they continued, "these cannot be brought to bear on every point, even of the surface of society." Notwithstanding the most vigorous efforts of the Bible societies, thousands remained "still destitute of the sacred volume." In spite of the most dedicated efforts of earnest pastors and scholars to develop pastors' training schools (and here men like Rice and Staughton spoke with the authority of experience), "the numbers and influence" of the clergy could not "be extended beyond a certain limit."

At the same time, tracts could be produced in great quantity and distributed with facility. They could convey "the pure truths of the Bible, recommended by the attractiveness of example, and the clearness of exposition, as well as enforced by exhortation." These founders of the Tract Society envisioned their printed testimonies reaching the environment where men lived daily: "in the steamboat," "at the tavern," "in the workshop," "at home." And if, perchance, the first invitation to come to Christ was disregarded by the reader, "the tract may remain at hand, to reproach him daily with his neglect and to warn him of his danger."

Another facet of the situation thrilled the founders. Being Baptists and thus sturdy advocates of soul liberty, individual responsibility, and the priesthood of all believers, they stressed the fact that tract distribution enabled "every man to become a preacher of righteousness." The traveler, the neighbor, the friend, and the tongue-tied mate could all become ambassadors of Christ.

In addition to these obvious reasons, a more subtle fact underlay the desire for a tract society. This was the inherent danger of fragmentation which ever accompanied religious groups following the congregational polity. Split-offs could occur in various directions. In the first part of the nineteenth century in America, Benjamin Randall had led his followers away from the moderate Calvinism followed by most Baptists of the time, while the hyper-Calvinists of the Primitive Baptist group were moving oppositely. Concerned Baptists were aroused by both agitations and they had reason to be. "It is desirable," said the founders, "to produce among the members of the denomination, a closer union than has yet subsisted." It was not an easy time to be a Baptist, as they freely admitted. "The leading design, which a portion of the denomination are labouring to effect, are regarded by other portions with indifference or disapprobation." Needless to say, the problems did not disappear with the rise of the new evangelistic effort, but much good was achieved and more unity was established. Moreover, this would not be the last time that Baptists would attempt to heal the divisions with the adhesive force of an overriding evangelistic effort.

Colporter Wagon

2. Focusing *the Witness*

From
Tract
Society
to
Publication
Society

With the foundations of the society quickly set, the momentum continued as the expansion into full service developed. More than merely being a printer of literature, the society was also in the business of promotion and distribution. Not content to sit back and wait for orders, the leaders made every effort to get those orders and then to get the people to read the printed page.

TRACT DEPOSITORIES

To distribute the tracts effectively, a system of depositories was developed. In the first year these were established at Hudson, New York; Philadelphia, Pennsylvania; Norfolk and Richmond, Virginia; Charleston, South Carolina; Augusta and Savannah, Georgia; and Marietta, Ohio. A decade later, the number had been increased to fifty-six, of which twenty-five were owned by the General Society and the remainder were locally sponsored. These depositories were essentially wholesale-retail stores to which the general printing house could forward its material and from which churches and agents could obtain needed supplies.

Financial support for any such endeavor is crucially important. For Baptists with their congregational polity this need offers unusual problems. A dedicated and farseeing group may plan a project, but continued effective support is essential if it is to succeed. Thus, a variety of means was adopted for raising funds. The tracts were sold as well as given away. In the first fifteen years of the society's life one hundred ministers became life directors by contributing $25 each, and three hundred became life members for a $10 fee. Female memberships for life were also welcomed and were segregated by name. There were less than one hundred in this group. Other life memberships, presumably held by laymen, were available at $10 "or upwards" and about two hundred were claimed. So between seven and eight hundred Baptists were supporters of the work on record in 1838, including most Baptists of distinction at that time.

EVANGELIZING IN MIDDLE AMERICA

Of great concern was the rapidly expanding population of the Mississippi Valley. Clearly seeing the challenge here, the leaders of the Tract Society in 1835 set out to raise a special fund of $5,000 to support a Christian literature campaign in that area. The approach was simple: enlist two hundred persons who would each pledge $5 per year for five years.

Three years later, the goal was almost reached, but by that time the plan had been enlarged to raise $10,000. On an annual budget of $10,000 or less an attempt was being made to win America for Christ. For extra measure, Burma and Germany were included also!

Baptists in those days thought of need first and means second. Indeed, much of the annual report for 1838 was devoted to testimonies on the value of the Mississippi Valley project. Brother Orr of Arkansas wrote: ". . . Permit me to say that they [the *Tracts* and *Manuals*] have been useful beyond my most sanguine expectation . . . a discordant mass of elements has been thrown together here, with every shade of religious sentiment from high toned Antinomianism down to sheer Arminianism."

Brother Gale of Tennessee apparently had a large constituency of antimissionary folk. He reported that the tract *Dialogue on Missions* was so greatly demanded that the supply was promptly exhausted.

Brother Logan of Illinois, feeling in a generous mood, furnished all the ministers in his area with a supply of tracts "for gratuitous distribution." He hoped that they would "prove a blessing."

Brother Bard of Ohio was a little more successful, businesswise. At the meeting of the Portage Association he presented "the cause" and was rewarded with 160 orders for the *Baptist Manual,* a handbook of 400 pages. His request to the printing house, however, was for 200 copies. Apparently he wanted to be prepared for additional orders.

A NEW NAME

The foregoing shows clearly that the activity of the society had gone far beyond the original limits and goals, and the time had arrived for a formal change in its scope and structure. In 1835, therefore, at a large gathering in Richmond, the suggestion was made "to have a Society to publish and circulate valuable books, particularly of a denominational character, for family use, Sunday Schools, etc." At that time it was the plan to urge the Tract Society to become that major publishing organization. This, in effect, was what the Society already was, but it took five years for the idea to set. By 1840 the Tract Society became the American Baptist Publication and Sunday School Society.

Under the expanded organization, several changes were to be effected:

—a new name;

—an enlarged publication schedule to include not only tracts but sabbath school books and volumes of a biographical, doctrinal, or historical nature "which publications shall embrace chiefly those of a denominational character";

—an agreement with the American Tract Society, the American Sunday School Union, and the New England Sunday School Union that their publications might be sold through Baptist agents and stores;

—an aggressive program of enlarging the list of depositories and agents for increased service and effectiveness.

JOHN MASON PECK

In addition to a new plan, there came upon the scene a new leader, the renowned John Mason Peck. The Reverend M. J. Rhees had been filling the position of corresponding secretary for the Society, but, with the development of organization and the accompanying need for a business agent more adept at traveling, he had resigned the position and assumed the pastorate of the Second Baptist Church, Wilmington, Delaware, and Peck was appointed in his place.

Peck, born in Litchfield, Connecticut, in 1789, was another spiritual son of Dr. Staughton. Under the advice of Luther Rice, the

John Mason Peck

Shurtleff College, founded by Peck
in 1827

young Peck, already engaged in mission work in New York State, had moved to Philadelphia to further his education under the direction of the great pastor and teacher. There, at the triennial meeting of the General Missionary Convention in 1817, Peck and his friend James E. Welch had been appointed as missionaries to the Missouri Territory, which was at that time frontier country presenting a great opportunity for the proclamation of the gospel. This experience was a great disappointment to Peck, however, for there was not enough Baptist money to support this work along with the Burma Mission and Columbian College. In his third year in the position he became ill with a fever which nearly took his life. His oldest son died, followed by his brother-in-law. The health of his wife was precarious. He was strapped for funds and worried about a growing family to support. Nevertheless, the obvious challenge of the situation encouraged him to remain at his post.

Two years later, the Massachusetts Baptist Missionary Society rallied to his support, and shortly thereafter he obtained a half-section of unimproved land near Rock Island, Illinois, which became his base of operations from then on. These "operations" were many. They included the founding of Shurtleff College, publication of a Baptist magazine, organization of the Illinois Baptist Education Society, giving aid in organizing the American Baptist Home Mission Society, superintending of Valley activities for the Publication Society, serving as fund raiser extraordinary, traveling as an evangelist, and helping to found in 1853 an Historical Department of the Publication Society (now back with the Board of Educational Ministries after years of a separate identity as the American Baptist Historical Society). No wonder Harvard University honored him with the doctorate!

As the life of John Peck illustrates, the two-fold thrust of the Baptists through their Publication Society was now even more plainly marked than at the beginning. Evangelism and education were both to be stressed, fulfilling the original objective, "to disseminate evangelical truth and to inculcate sound morals. . . ."

As pioneer pastors and missionaries tirelessly went about preaching, distributing tracts, exhorting sinners to be saved and saints to be sanctified, they also were bravely starting colleges, pastoral training schools, Sunday schools, and religious journals.

In a general circular prepared by Peck on behalf of the Publication Society, these aims were given wide distribution. In this document the author stated that the paramount object of the Society was "to make our denomination . . . a reading, thinking, working, and devoutly religious people." To this end, "sound doctrine must be taught," and "the duties of the Christian profession . . . must be understood. . . ." The Society proposed four means of implementation:

1. the free distribution of religious tracts;
2. the publication (or purchase) and distribution by sale, at low prices, of religious books for family and general reading;
3. the providing of ministers with small and select libraries of a professional nature (It was estimated that at least *two thousand* pastors were in great need in this regard.);
4. the aiding of Sunday schools and Bible classes through encouragement and the supply of books and materials.

NEW HAMPSHIRE CONFESSION

These Baptists 150 years ago believed that they had a distinctive message, but there was no unanimity as to what that message was. One who helped provide a widely accepted definition of that message and, even more, who was extremely influential in its dissemination was Rev. J. Newton Brown, a native of New London, Connecticut, and a graduate of Hamilton College (now Colgate). Brown was pastor of the church at Exeter, New Hampshire, when the Baptists of the area were going through an agonizing reappraisal of their theology. The Free Will message was forcing some modification of the more traditional Calvinism. How could the Baptist thought-form be recast to fulfill changing concepts of identity and integrity?

The New Hampshire State Convention in 1830 appointed a committee to address itself to this task and to prepare "such a Declaration of Faith and Practice, together with a Covenant, as may be thought agreeable and consistent with the views of all our churches in this State." The idea of a Baptist confession of faith was by no means new; English and continental Baptists had created several in the past, and the Philadelphia Confession (1742) had been an influential force among American Baptists. However, Brown felt that the time was ripe for a new one which reflected the changing theology of the times. As a result Baron Stow, a founder of the Publication Society; Jonathan Going, a founder of the American Baptist Home Mission Society and later president of Denison University, together with Brown finally brought together a suitable draft of a statement which was presented to the New Hampshire Convention's Board on

Jonathan Going, pastor of First Baptist Church, Worcester, Massachusetts, and supporter of John Mason Peck

January 15, 1833. It was approved "after slight alterations" and was recommended to the churches for adoption.

Some have said that this Confession of Faith "might never have been known outside of New Hampshire except for the work of J. Newton Brown." Be that as it may, Brown did become editor of the American Baptist Publication Society in 1849, and four years later, included it in a new edition of the popular *Baptist Manual.* This confession became a theological guide for thousands of churches and helped greatly to popularize the "landmark" movement among Baptists which heavily stressed theological orthodoxy and the independence of the local church. For years the New Hampshire Confession of Faith, though having no official standing, has been one of the doctrinal guideposts used by evangelicals in American Baptist churches in their search for theological integrity.

Christian literature was distributed by colporters, traveling on foot, by horse and wagon, and later by automobile. Notice the man at the far right of the picture at the bottom of page 33. He is using a yoke across his neck and shoulders to carry his supply cases. The term "colporter" is derived from this practice—"col" meaning neck and "porter" meaning carry.

THE COLPORTERS

Baptists by 1843 numbered 700,000 members, with a rate of growth that doubled every twelve years. Thus the pressure for adequate instructional tools came from the cry of man as well as from the call of God. To accomplish this commission, the Society appealed for money to employ one hundred Baptist ministers as colporters, furnish each with $300 worth of books for sale and distribution, pay each a modest wage for support, and turn them loose to visit "associations, churches, Sunday schools, and families." It would be the business of these colporters to distribute Christian literature and to "preach the Gospel to the destitute, inculcate habits of reading, sober thought and devout practice." The idea had originated with French reformers, centuries before, who operated a Bible and Christian tract society out of Basel, Switzerland, and traveled about the countryside witnessing for Christ, carrying their supplies in the common shoulder harness slings used by the peasants of the day. Thus, two old French words—*col* "neck" and *porter* "carry"— combined with an old Swiss custom to become a new American idea in evangelism.

The scheme included the idea of a nominal salary, plus a commission from sales, allowing the development of a rather extensive sales staff at a modest capital outlay. In 1854, there were 62 colporters; two years later, 109. Some worked for many years, others briefly.

The schedule of activities of these itinerant missionaries and booksellers is suggested by reports of Rev. A. B. Harris. He worked in Illinois, Missouri, and Kentucky in the 1840s traveling 2,486 miles during one six-month period, visiting 40 churches, contacting 275 families, preaching 66 sermons, delivering 28 other addresses, selling 644 books, and distributing 9,000 pages of tracts! For this, he received a salary of $75 and expenses of $27.12, part of which paid the freight on books sent him. Clearly, the profession of colporter was not designed to make one rich! But for one hundred years, these were among the most intrepid of front-line troops in the mission of the churches.

EDUCATION IN THE SOUTH

The tragic conflict known as the Civil War came and went, leaving a trail of destruction and grief. Out of it, however, some positive results came, including a reaffirmation of the Federal Union and the beginning of a new era for the Black man. Up to this time education for Negroes had been largely unavailable; in fact, in many areas it had been illegal to teach a slave to read. Now, however, Baptists became actively concerned.

In its 1865 report, the Publication Society clearly recognized the problem. The people "must be taught to read." Books were needed; so a *First Reader for Freedman* was issued. It contained "a picture alphabet, spelling lessons, and fifty-two short reading lessons." "The promotion of the spiritual welfare of those taught" was not neglected. It was understood that as soon as the ability to read was achieved, instruction "in the principles of the gospel" would proceed. Thus the Society followed the teaching of the sixteenth-century Reformers, who said that the common man must learn to read in order that he may read the Bible! The *First Reader* was followed by *The Freedman's Book of Christian Doctrine.* In thousands of Sunday schools which were being organized among those newly freed from bondage, materials for religious instruction were furnished, often at no cost, by the Society.

LESSON HELPS

The freedmen of the South were not the only ones helped by a new thrust in Christian education. By the close of the Civil War the Sunday school movement was, roughly, fifty years old. More importantly the growth of population, especially in cities, and the improvement of roads and transportation allowed large groups to gather regularly in one place for a comparatively short period of time. Here arose a natural demand for Sunday school literature on a vast scale.

Leading in the effort to produce educational materials suitable for this growing group of students and teachers were the Reverend John H. Vincent, a Methodist minister and founder of the Chautauqua Assembly, and B. F. Jacobs, a produce merchant and the Sunday school superintendent at Chicago's First Baptist Church. Combining their talents, the two made a remarkable team. Faced with massed enrollments (over a thousand at First Baptist), these men devised the idea of "uniform lessons" whereby "helps" would be furnished to both pupils and teachers of all age levels on the same subject at the same time. The uniform approach would allow the broadest coverage by the finest scholars at the least cost. It would allow the publishing houses, still modest enterprises, to meet the tremendous challenge.

The American Baptist Publication Society was alert to this movement and began publishing a series of lessons in 1870 "for every Lord's Day in the month." The circulation was over 50,000 the first year.

The idea caught on rapidly, with various publishers entering the field. Cooperation was clearly called for at this point. So it was that Mr. Jacobs at the National Sunday School Convention in 1872 in Indianapolis called for one International Lesson Committee to prepare themes and texts to be used uniformly by the several denominations. The idea was adopted with "only ten voting in the negative" out of a vast crowd of delegates.

LEADERS

Emerson's remark that "an institution is the lengthened shadow of one man" can be applied with some enlargement to the Publication Society. At the outset, it was the inspiration and energy of a few men who brought the organization into being. Then, as the work grew and expanded, it was still a small group of dedicated people who carried the burden. In more than a limited sense, it was the endeavor of one family—the Crozers.

John Price Crozer was born in Springfield, Pennsylvania, in 1793 and at the age of fourteen was baptized in the Schuylkill River "at the end of Spruce Street" by the noted Dr. Staughton. Paternal bereavement, poverty, and vicissitude characterized Crozer's youth, but by dint "of hard work and strict economy" his fortune began to turn for the better. Eventually, as owner and manager of large textile mills in Chester, Pennsylvania, he became a man of wealth and substance. Still, his Christian commitment never faded. At the age of fifty-five he could write, "I feel the utter worthlessness of riches, and yet all the time to be making haste to be rich is a feature in human nature, or at least in mine." This character of introspection was not a minor note with Crozer. The next year he wrote, "Would to God I might be directed to some field of enlarged usefulness, in which no self-interest could ensue!"

Dr. Staughton's convert did not have to look far to find fulfillment of his ardent prayer. He built a Baptist church at nearby Upland, endowed a number of Baptist churches in the Chester area, gave munificent benefactions to the University of Lewisburg (later named Bucknell University for his son-in-law, William Bucknell), and became associated with the Publication Society. Through the latter,

36

he established a Sunday school library fund of $10,000 and a ministers' library fund of $5,000. Following his death in 1866, his family established a missionary memorial fund of $50,000 to be used by the Society for its work in the South and, climaxing all other gifts, gave $275,000 for the endowment of Crozer Theological Seminary. These were all major gifts, particularly by the standards of a hundred years ago. Surely they gave American Baptists through publication and educational efforts a remarkable measure of strength not possible otherwise.

William Bucknell was born near the Crozer place southeast of Philadelphia. He was a wood-carver by trade. In this practice he was so successful that he soon had gathered a small amount of capital which he put to judicious use, first in brokerage and real-estate transactions, and then in major construction projects, including municipal gas and water works. He became a member of the board of managers of the Publication Society in 1841 at the age of thirty and continued to serve in this capacity until his death in 1890. During twenty-three of those forty-nine years he served as chairman. It was stated after his death that he had been "the largest single giver to The American Baptist Publication Society."

Benjamin Griffith was another of the Crozer clan who became active and influential in the life of the Society. He was thirty-three years of age and pastor of one of the leading churches of Philadelphia, Fourth Baptist, when he married Elizabeth Crozer, daughter of the aforementioned John. Three years later, in 1857, Griffith became the executive officer of the Society. He had already been a member of the board for several years and active in some of its most delicate negotiations, including chairman of the committee appointed to "designate the duties of the secretaries," chairman of the publishing-fund committee, and chief liaison person arranging the merger of the New England Sabbath School Union into the Publication Society.

The second half of the century was a difficult time for the Baptist publishing house. The surge of enthusiasm for missionary effort in the Mississippi Valley had ebbed after a great advance. The country had suffered a serious financial depression in the 1870s and was badly divided over the slavery question. Baptists were weakened by the schism over slavery in 1845. Not the least of troubles came through the resignation of several key staff persons and the death in 1857 of such an important life member as William Colgate. Clearly the call

AMERICAN BAPTIST PUBLICATION SOCIETY

PHILADELPHIA
BIBLE
HOUSE

530

AMERICAN
BAPTIST
PUBLICATION
SOCIETY.

Offices at 530 Arch Street, Philadelphia, 1850–1876

Crozer Building at 1420 Chestnut Street, Philadelphia

was for a vigorous administrator. In the previous thirty-three years of its history, the average term of office for corresponding secretary had been three years. Griffith changed that. He served from 1857 until 1893—thirty-six years!

A NEW HOME

Nowhere did the administrative drive and talent of Dr. Griffith become more evident than in the erection of the new home of the Society at 1420 Chestnut Street, Philadelphia. The original move from Washington to Philadelphia had been effected in 1826 over the strenuous objections of Luther Rice, who sought to make the nation's capital a center of Baptist activity and interest. The idea was sound, but the circumstances were not. The capital city at that time was only the political center of the country. Transportation, finance, commerce, education, and the publishing business were concentrated elsewhere. Philadelphia was a natural choice for the Society's home.

At first the headquarters had been established in a second-floor room near the corner of Front and Market Streets at a rent of $100 per year. The second home of the Society was even more modest—a few shelves in David Clark's bookstore at 118 North Fourth Street. After a year and a half, a place on the northwest corner of Fifth and North Streets was taken, then at 21 South Fourth, followed by another at 31 North Sixth, and then in 1850 a building at 118 Arch Street was purchased. Enlarged, refurbished, rebuilt, and renumbered (becoming 530 Arch Street) this humble building served as the home of the Society for twenty-six years.

A more adequate building for the headquarters of the Society was needed, but little could be done until after the crisis of the Civil War and after the surge of missionary expansion in the West and South. Quietly, funds began to accumulate. Bucknell started the drive with a gift of $25,000, which he later doubled. Other members of his family added enough to increase the sum to $77,550. Other relatives among the Crozers contributed $92,000. Eighty-seven additional donors supplied nearly $60,000. The old property on Arch Street was sold for almost $30,000. With this total of about $260,000 a property at 1420 Chestnut Street was acquired and a commodious and attractive five-story building was erected, debt free.

The design, claimed the Board in its initial report (1876), had "an air of simple, quiet elegance." Four stories fronting on Chestnut Street were of "pure white marble." The fifth story was a "mansard roof, covered with slate." There was a passenger elevator worked by steam power. Also, there were a freight elevator, a dumbwaiter, speaking tubes, water piped to each floor, and "separate dressingrooms on each floor for ladies and gentlemen." These all contributed justifiably to an aura of success. In 1850 there were receipts of $14,972 for benevolence and $42,146 accrued from business operations. By 1876 these items had increased under Dr. Griffith's able administration to $62,000 and $490,364 respectively. Whereas the first annual report had showed an income of $373, a half century later it was well over half a million dollars. Truly, the American Baptist Publication Society had arrived!

Printing Plant at Juniper and Lombard Streets, Philadelphia, dedicated in 1896

3. Developing the Witnes

The
Society's
Second
Half
Century

The first fifty years of the Publication Society's life had been exciting times of establishment. The new had been tried and found not wanting. A new organization had been born and it had lived, vigorously. A new method had been tried and it had worked. Christian literature was flowing from the presses in an ever-increasing stream—46,643,059 pieces in the decade of 1864–1874. Families were being paid evangelistic calls; people were being won to Christ; and Sunday schools were being organized—about six thousand during a forty-year period. Progress had been made from one man carrying tracts in a top hat to a thoroughly organized business institution occupying its own headquarters in a new five-story structure in a prime location in America's second largest city.

The witness had unquestionably been established. As the Society entered its second half century of service, the task was to make full use of the talent and technique which had been brought together. Developing the witness was now the task, and to this end the redoubtable Dr. Benjamin Griffith and the sagacious Dr. A. J. Rowland, who between them served as chief executive officers of the Society for fifty-seven years, set themselves. Advance was directed on six fronts: education, particularly in the local church; evangelism,

LESSON XII. MARCH 18.
THE SON REJECTED.

He came unto his own, and his own received him not. John i. 11.

GOLDEN TEXT

LESSON HYMN
6s. 5s.
Jesus, meek and gentle,
Son of God, most high,
Pitying, loving Saviour,
Hear thy children's cry;
Though so long rejected,
Fill our hearts with love;
Draw us, holy Jesus,
To thy home above.

REMEMBER
Do I send Jesus away without all that belongs to him?

Church school material
produced in 1888

LESSON III. Jan. 15.
Jesus Walking
on the Sea.

GOLDEN TEXT

BE OF GOOD CHEER; IT IS I; BE
NOT AFRAID. Matt. xiv. 27.

REMEMBER
If in danger, for
Trusting Jesus

LESSON HYMN
8s.
Pass me not, O pre
When the storm
In the danger, i
At my side be

44

featured by the railway chapel car; Bible publication; social action, especially through temperance education; unification of effort within the denomination and with like-minded folk in other groups, some Baptist and some not; and enlarging and strengthening the central business organization.

EDUCATION

The Publication Society, said Dr. Griffith on one occasion, is "prominently a Sunday school Society." Considering the source of the remark, it is not surprising to find that Sunday school work was demanding more and more attention as the years of the nineteenth century wore on. The American Sunday school was very different from that begun in Gloucester, England, nearly a century earlier by Robert Raikes to bring the children in from the streets and give them some basic education on the one day they were not employed. A rising tide of support for public schools and of opposition to child labor had combined to allow the Sunday church school in the United States to become more strictly a religious institution than its English predecessor.

One of the first and fullest statements of standards for Sunday school literature was that presented by the Publishing Committee of the Publication Society's Board in 1886. Although its immediate application was to books for church libraries, the implication for Sunday school materials in general was too clear to miss. Until well into the twentieth century the principles then outlined were to be determinative in shaping American Baptist Christian education materials:

1. They should have a direct and special bearing on the great end of Sunday school teaching.
2. In their presentation of the gospel, they should be clear and distinct; their teaching to correspond fully with the teachings of the sacred Scriptures, presenting always the blood of Christ as the only ground of a sinner's acceptance with God, and faith in Christ as the inquirer's first and immediate duty.
3. Every statement in regard to biblical subjects should be able to bear the test of the most full and accurate study of the Word of God.
4. Books which have no relation to the special end of the Sunday school should not be placed in its library.
5. Works of fiction should be examined with great care, and none

should be admitted unless they can bear the test of a wise and thorough scrutiny. It is a greater evil to have too many than it is to admit too few of this class of works.

6. In order to give opportunity for such careful examination as has been indicated, it is desirable that the additions to the library should be made gradually.

As the twentieth century opened, other ideas began to permeate education. The one-room school was disappearing and being supplanted by the graded school. Educational levels were rising with the development of public high schools and mass enrollments. The long popularity of the McGuffey Readers was over. Shortly, publishers would be reprinting them as curios. State laws on school standards would become vastly more detailed and comprehensive.

This spirit of the times was not lost on those active in the Sunday school movement. A glance at *The Baptist Sunday School Standard Manual* (1917) shows the powerful influence which secular education had brought to the religious school. Several items were listed:

Extension—there should be a cradle roll, a home department, and a new members' canvass.

Membership—average attendance should equal 60 percent of the enrollment.

Enrollment—should equal church membership.

Reports—ought to be filed annually at denominational headquarters.

Grading of classes—should be sharply divided as to age and with annual promotions.

Evangelism—there was to be definite instruction on this with an opportunity for the pupils to accept Christ as Savior.

Organized classes among adults were to be encouraged and certificates of recognition given for achievement.

Courses in teacher training were to be offered through the local church, summer assemblies, or correspondence study.

Workers' conferences were to be held "at least monthly," and there was to be an official committee on religious education.

Missions and temperance—special instruction was to be given.

Weekly offerings were to cover expenses.

Special days were to be Children's Day and Rally Day.

This program would surely result in a school far different from the one led by John Wanamaker in Philadelphia, which by the turn of the century was one of the largest in the world; yet it was already outmoded. Wanamaker's gathering of a thousand or two thousand —children, youth, and adults all crowded into one huge hall, each group of eight or ten clustered about a single teacher, each talking about the same lesson—was not what the new educators had in mind.

In the 1890s William R. Harper, president of the University of Chicago and noted Hebrew scholar, conceived the plan of providing a series of textbooks for the study of the Bible, which should be adopted for all ages, to meet the needs of several periods of life from kindergarten to adulthood. This idea was put into action through a series of publications known as the Blakeslee Graded Lessons, issued by the University of Chicago Press. By 1908, the plan had the enthusiastic approval of the International Sunday School Association, headed by W. N. Hartshorn, a longtime superintendent of the school for Ruggles Street Baptist Church, Boston.

Among others intrigued by the new approach was Dr. C. R. Blackall. A native of Albany, New York, and a graduate of Rush Medical College in Chicago, he had served as a surgeon during the Civil War with the 33rd Regiment from Wisconsin. Resigning this post in 1864, he had returned to Chicago and entered the field of Christian education in cooperation with B. F. Jacobs, D. L. Moody, and others. In 1867, Dr. Blackall accepted appointment as district secretary for the American Baptist Publication Society, and for fifty-seven years until his death in 1924 he maintained some official connection with the Society.

As editor of *Our Little Ones* from 1873 and editor-in-chief of all Sunday school periodicals for the Society from 1882, Dr. Blackall was in a position to observe and evaluate the Chicago experiment. As a result the Keystone Graded Lessons were introduced in 1909. These new lessons, said Dr. Blackall, were "written by Baptists, and in accord with Baptist views of truth." At the same time, he insisted that they also were "in line with the most recent studies of child life and Sunday school pedagogy, and are of the highest mechanical excellence."

EVANGELISM

Another notable innovation by the Baptist Publication Society was the chapel car. The Reverend Dr. Wayland Hoyt was pastor of the First Baptist Church, Minneapolis; his brother, Colgate, was a leading railroad magnate and, as such, the possessor of his own private car. These two, together with a Sunday school missionary with the improbable name of Boston W. Smith, were the originators of the idea. Blueprints were drawn of a railroad car providing for living quarters, an office, and a tiny chapel. This would allow for a missionary and his wife to move into any new community served by a railroad and be ready to work with dignity and stability in the shortest possible time. The day of the roughriding evangelist who

Mr. and Mrs. Howard Parry at home in the Chape

Railroad-center workers gat
for worship in a Chap

Chapel Car *Grace* on a siding in Utah

Service in Chapel Car *Grace* en route to Green Lake

often had to fight the town bully before he could hold his first meeting was over.

The plan developed swiftly. Within a year from conception, the first car, *Evangel,* was dedicated at Cincinnati in 1891. Pushed by the Chapel Car Syndicate in New York, composed of men like John D. Rockefeller, Charles L. Colby, John R. Trevor, James B. Colgate, E. J. Barney, and William Hills, who furnished financial and moral support, the movement quickly grew. Soon *Emmanuel, Glad Tidings, Good Will, Messenger of Peace, Herald of Hope,* and *Grace* joined *Evangel* to make a substantial group of ready-made Pullman chapel cars for service throughout the West. In half a century of chapel-car service, hundreds of communities were enabled to have Sunday schools, vacation schools, Bible classes, evangelistic meetings, and organized churches which might not otherwise have been possible. The lasting marks made by the chapel-car missionaries lie mainly, of course, in the changed lives of the thousand people to whom they ministered. Further evidence is furnished by the towns that sprang up, such as Hermiston, Oregon, named for missionary E. R. Hermiston, or the great churches that grew from seeds planted by the railroad ministry, such as the First Baptist Church, Van Nuys, California, which was started in 1911 and is now claimed to be the largest Baptist church "west of Texas." One of the chapel cars, *Grace,* is still preserved at the American Baptist Assembly in Green Lake, Wisconsin.

As companions to the chapel cars in the vehicle vanguard for Christ were the colportage wagons (first used in Michigan in the 1890s) and the chapel-car autos (first used in 1923). The latter were really large buses equipped with living quarters and a small office or reception room. A trailer carried a tent which could be attached to the rear of the bus allowing for a congregation of about one hundred to be seated. The pulpit was revealed as the back door of the bus opened. The organ was the gift of the Estey Organ Company of Vermont, and the gas lanterns were from the Coleman Company of Kansas.

Another unique method of conveyance used by the colporters was the gospel cruiser. This was a boat fitted out somewhat as the chapel cars and buses, but with appropriate adjustments for marine use. Such cruisers were employed along the waterways of the coast from California to Alaska. With land transportation extremely difficult because of the mountainous terrain, and with air service yet to come, many communities were dependent upon ships for commerce and

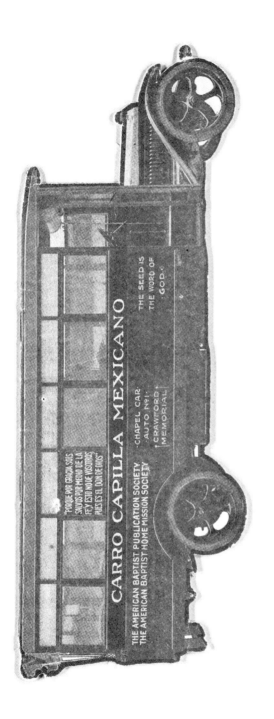

Chapel Car auto used in Spanish American ministry

supplies of all kinds. Into this situation, the gospel cruiser fitted splendidly.

When one considers the generation of the chapel car, the colporter bus, and the gospel cruiser, one can only be amazed at the energy and ingenuity of those responsible for such unusual, yet practical, means of multiplying the witness. A sturdy Baptist church stands today in a thriving town in eastern Washington State in part because the chapel car, *Messenger of Peace,* came with Rev. and Mrs. Robert Gray. Would the First Baptist Church of Sunnyside, Washington, have lived had it not been for the colporter? Who knows? But the fact is that these events did occur.

In its evangelistic work, the Publication Society quickly found itself involved not only with people of the majority Anglo-Saxon stock, but also with growing minority groups. This broad concern for persons had been present with the Society from the beginning. Some of its earliest publications had been for the use of Judson and his mission to Burma. Europe also had been an area of service. One of the earliest major appropriations had occurred in 1826 when $300 was allotted to a Rev. Jonas King "to be employed in procuring translations of this Society's Tracts into the language of modern Greece" and to be distributed by him in that country.

Better known is the effort on behalf of the Germans. Led to the Baptist position through the reading of a few of the Society's tracts, John Oncken had converted several persons and in 1834 was immersed with seven others at Hamburg, Germany, by Dr. Sears of Colgate University, Hamilton, New York. A Baptist church was established with Oncken as pastor. The witness continued to multiply under this dynamic leadership. American Baptist publications were translated, and under American Baptist auspices a German Baptist publishing house was founded, which today continues in altered form under the name Oncken Verlag. For forty years John Oncken led this pioneer effort in an ancient land. In 1876, the Society was so convinced of the worth of the Baptist witness in continental Europe that it commissioned Philip W. Bickel to succeed Oncken as manager of the publishing house. From this tiny center of Baptist influence, gospel light radiated into many areas, particularly Scandinavia and Eastern Europe.

The work in America among the newly arrived had been equally thrilling. The Reverend Conrad A. Fleischmann began preaching among his fellow Germans in 1839, first in New York, then in New

Jersey and Pennsylvania. For years he served as editor of the *General Conference German Baptist Journal.* The Fleischmann Memorial Baptist Church of Philadelphia helps keep alive his memory today. Among the Swedish people, one remembers Andreas Wiberg, a missionary of the Society and a founder among the Swedish Baptists, both in Europe and America. His first position after marriage was as "superintendent of colportage in Sweden at a salary of six hundred dollars a year, under the auspices of the American Baptist Publication Society."

What shall be said of work among the many other bilingual and ethnic groups who had streamed into the United States during the first century of the Publication Society's life? They had come from everywhere. They had come with all sorts of needs, not the least of which was a knowledge of the gospel and of the Bible in their own language. The former would be explained through literature published by American Baptists and distributed by colporters commissioned by American Baptists. During 1912, a typical year, there were one hundred colporters employed, forty of whom worked among non-English-speaking people. Scriptures, as often as not, would be supplied by these American Baptist missionaries either through their own publishing house or in cooperation with others. The Word *would* get around.

THE SCRIPTURES

It is difficult in this age of ecumenism and new Bible translations to understand the problems raised in the minds of our forefathers regarding cooperative publication of the Scriptures, but in fact serious difficulties did arise. Among Baptists, trouble arose over the translation of the New Testament Greek word *baptizo.* It means "to dip, immerse." They wanted the word translated so that their mode of baptism by immersion would be clearly substantiated. It was on this point that the early Baptists made issue with existing Bible translations.

Baptists, however, were never solidly sectarian in polity and usually found themselves working in normal harmony with Christians of other groupings on a wide variety of projects. So it was that when Carey went to India and Judson to Burma and when their translations of the Bible began to come forth, Christians of many denominations became involved in the enterprise. The British Bible Society (established in 1804) "begged the privilege" of handling monies being raised for Carey's Bible publication. The American Bible Society (established in 1816) gave financial support to the publication of the Burmese Bible by Judson. Baptists, of course, were active in both societies and these were natural and wonderful outlets of energy.

Problems arose, however, when the pedobaptists (believers in infant baptism) in the Bible Societies learned that the Greek word *baptizo* was being translated in accord with Baptist teachings. Disturbed that the churches on the mission field would become immersionist, they caused a cancellation of support and thus forced a change in the translation. This only aroused Baptists to greater effort. Led by such stalwarts as Spencer Cone, later pastor of the first Baptist Church, New York; Jonathan Going, corresponding secretary of the American Baptist Home Mission Society; and William Colgate and William Judd, laymen, they formed an organization called the American and Foreign Bible Society. In its second year of life, the new Society reported that $43,823 had been received and that the Scriptures were being circulated in twenty-six languages.

The matter was not ended, however. Baptists are quite adept at finding new problems, or new questions to old problems. If it was unwise to allow the word *baptizo* to be simply transliterated from the Greek into Burmese as "baptize," is it not also unwise to allow the same thing in English? If "immerse" is the proper translation, why not use it? For fourteen years Baptists debated these questions among themselves, but to no consensus. Finally, the American Bible Union began in 1850 as an offshoot of the American and Foreign Bible Society with the avowed purpose "to procure and circulate the most faithful versions of the Sacred Scriptures in all languages throughout the world." It raised more than a million dollars. Long before other major revisions appeared (The English Revised in 1885 and the American Standard in 1901), the Bible Union had published its immersionist translations of the Scriptures.

The result of all this was to have two Baptist Bible Societies, as well as the Publication Society, in the business of producing and distributing the Holy Scriptures. It was a situation crying for attention. Meetings looking toward merger or coordination were held from 1859 onward. Progress was minimal until 1883, when at Saratoga, New York, the three groups came to an understanding and decided that "the Bible work of Baptists should be done by our two existing Societies—the foreign work by the American Baptist Missionary Union and the home work by the American Baptist Publication Society" (These are now known as the Board of International Ministries and the Board of Educational Ministries of the American Baptist Churches in the U.S.A.). Even before the official union, the three groups had cooperated with each other. As early as 1865, for instance, the Publication Society had engaged three outstanding scholars to take the new Bible Union version and "subject it to careful revision." This Improved Edition of the New Testament was introduced in 1891 and was done by Dr. Alvah Hovey, president of Newton Theological Institution; Dr. Henry G. Weston, president of Crozer Theological Seminary; and Dr. John A. Broadus, professor of New Testament at Southern Baptist Theological Seminary. In 1889 the task of revising the Bible Union's Old Testament work was assigned to Dr. B.C. Taylor, then of Crozer Seminary and later a member of the faculty of Eastern Seminary; Dr. William R. Harper and Dr. I. M. Price of the University of Chicago; and Dr. John R. Sampey, professor of Old Testament and later president of Southern Baptist Seminary. The work begun in 1865 was finally completed in 1912 with the appearance of the whole Improved Edition Bible.

After such struggles of administrators and scholars to produce a "Baptist" Bible, it might have been predicted that the presses would have been kept busy producing the new version for the satisfaction of the Baptist contituency. This did not happen. Most Baptists never heard of it.

A much more popular effort in Bible translation came from a more unexpected source—Helen Barrett Montgomery, the daughter of a classics scholar, the wife of a successful businessman, a founder of the World Day of Prayer (1919), and the first woman president of the Northern (later named American) Baptist Convention (1921). Mrs. Montgomery brought out her own translation of the New Testament in 1924 in celebration of the centennial anniversary of the American Baptist Publication Society. Over the years it has become a favorite of many Bible students even though it does use "baptize" instead of "immerse."

UNITY

From the foregoing account of the long struggle concerning Bible publications, it is evident that a low degree of unity existed among nineteenth-century Baptists. In the early part of the century the South and North had been one, with an ample share of leadership and support for the Publication Society coming from Southern sources. This broadly based foundation had continued until the schism over slavery in 1845. Even then, however, the issue did not become clearcut. Tightly structured and disciplined units were not integral to Baptist thought, a factor which became thoroughly apparent in the matter of Sunday school promotion and publication.

The Southern Baptist Publication Society had been organized in 1854 and the Southern Sunday School Union in 1858, both of them without denominational affiliation. Also there had been a group known as the Bible Board founded in 1851, which had become embroiled in the Landmark (theological isolation) controversy and had survived only ten years. Out of these movements a pressure developed for a Southern Baptist organization devoted to education and publication. As a result the Sunday School Board was created by the Southern Baptist Convention at Greenville, South Carolina, in 1863 and was soon merged with the Southern Baptist Publication Society to form the Sunday School and Publication Board.

These various Southern attempts at supporting Christian education did not receive unanimous cooperation from the Southern churches. Many continued to do business with the American Baptist Publication Society. The result of this, of course, was confusion and conflict between North and South. Conferences were held. Conversations were conducted. Correspondence was exchanged. Most ended as the one in 1889 reported: "We also had a conference, full and free, with the representatives of the American Baptist Publication Society, and we were unable to arrive at any agreement." The ABPS material was good, up-to-date, well produced and promoted; its supply houses were convenient; and the content was thoroughly Baptistic and free of the stain of schismatic Landmarkism. So many southern churches continued to do business with the Northerners. And good business it was—up to $50,000 a year. This the Society was not anxious to relinquish, especially in view of the growth potential in the expanding South.

The turning point came at the Southern Convention in Wilmington, North Carolina, in 1897, when Rev. J. M. Robertson, a Texan who was district secretary for the ABPS in the Southwest, made an open attack upon the struggling Sunday School Board. This united its friends, discomfited its enemies, and rescued the Board from oblivion. At that time the Society had approximately 250 workers throughout the South, nearly one-fourth of the staff. Needless to say, this number declined rapidly and by 1924 was only a remnant. By 1969, the Sunday School Board of the Southern Convention, which had been so maligned in 1897, was doing a thirty-five million dollar a year business.

Much more successful in outcome, but nearly as torturous in negotiation, was the understanding the Publication Society achieved with the American Baptist Home Mission Society. The Mission Society was only eight years younger than the Publication Society, and some of the same people were active in both. They served the same constituency. One was designed to promote the gospel through the printed page and the educational process; the other through the local church and the evangelistic process. In actual practice, however, the boundaries could not so easily be defined or maintained. The problem lay in the fact that the local church is one body and the individual Christian is one person. Educational and evangelistic forces may emanate from a variety of sources, but they unite in one being.

In 1874 the Board of the Publication Society found the situation so pressing that it attempted to spell out the differences and distinctions between itself and the ABHMS. It stated that the one was a "Church Missionary Society" and the other was a "Family and Sunday-school Missionary Society." As such, the latter would preach the gospel "from house to house," circulate the Holy Scriptures, form new Sunday schools, strengthen established schools, supply libraries for pastors, and, of course, publish the material to be used in all of this.

Though this definition seemed clear enough on the surface, in practice the confusion continued. Beginning in 1899 there was a continuing effort through meetings, formal and informal, to delineate the responsibilities. Through the next two decades the matter would require much attention. By 1918 the Northern Baptist Convention, which had been including the issue on its agenda regularly since 1910, reached the conclusion that the two Societies had different roles to play and could not be merged. The strong implication was that they ought to settle their own affairs. And this was done, with pomp and circumstance, on October 24, 1918. The two boards met at the Union League in Philadelphia and there, amid the solid splendor of a businessmen's club, agreements were reached. How much credit should accrue to the aura of affluence, the satisfaction of a delightful

Entrance to Roger Williams Building, 1703 Chestnut Street, Philadelphia

dinner, and the patina of patriotism ("flags of the Allies adorned the center of the great table") is not revealed in the recording documents. It is a fact, nevertheless, that the Publication Society agreed to relinquish its colporter system and its social service work to the Home Mission Society. It would continue to support these activities with funds and with administrative direction, but the Home Mission Society was to be the "agent."

Perhaps it was wise for the Publication Society to deemphasize its missionary responsibilities and concentrate more upon the printed word. Perhaps the resulting harmony was worth the cost. Certainly evangelism and social action were not forgotten by the educators. Certainly the Home Mission Society earnestly endeavored to fulfill its share of the bargain. Nevertheless, a corner was turned.

Among other areas in Christian unity which commanded attention from the leaders of the Publication Society were the formation of the Northern Baptist Convention, the incorporation of the Free Baptist group, and the development of interdenominational organizations of religious education. It was during the May, 1903, meeting of the several agencies of American Baptists in session at Buffalo, New York, that Dr. A. J. Rowland, executive officer of the Publication Society, offered a resolution to effect the annual assembly of the several societies "as one council or body." From this action came the formation four years later in Washington of the Northern Baptist Convention, later the American Baptist Churches in the U.S.A. Coincidentally in the year of the Convention's founding, 1907, the Publication Society sold its Crozer Building headquarters in Philadelphia at a profit and erected the Roger Williams Building two blocks up Chestnut Street. This was its home until the move to Valley Forge in 1962.

The spirit of interdenominational cooperation has always been a feature of American Baptist life. In the first report of the Society in 1825, the directors stated that they held "a fraternal regard for other Tract Societies" and that they did not enter the field of religious journalism "as a rival." Through cooperation over the years with the American Tract Society, the American Sunday School Union, and the various denominations this has been amply proved. The Society has been an active member of the Sunday School Council of the evangelical denominations, the World's Sunday School Association, the International Sunday School Association, and the International Council of Religious Education which became incorporated in the

National Council of Churches in 1950. The ABC is presently a member of the National Council, though a number of member churches exercise the option to restrict their ABC contributions from NCC support.

THEOLOGY

While the Publication Society was making great strides forward in publishing and business and in evangelism and education, new issues concerning Christian doctrine were arising.

The new thought stemmed mainly from the German rationalism of the nineteenth century, and most especially from Schleiermacher, who viewed the Christian faith not as objective but as subjective. Kenneth Scott Latourette, a great Baptist historian of a later day, said of him, "To many he seemed to make the Christian faith compatible with the thought forms of the day and therefore acceptable to honest minds" *(A History of Christianity, p. 1124)*. Another of the rationalists was F. C. Baur, who applied the Hegelian idea of thesis-antithesis-synthesis to the concepts of the New Testament with resulting distress to the preachers of traditional Christianity. Still another was D. F. Strauss, who raised the issue of myth with regard to the gospel record and left in historical doubt certain cardinal tenets of the faith, such as the virgin birth, the miracles, the atonement on the cross, the physical resurrection, and the Second Coming of Christ.

It must be emphasized that these and numerous others of their kind were not vicious enemies of the church attacking her sanctuary from without. These were confessing Christians and scholars of the highest repute attempting to make theology relevant to the growing sophisticated minds of the day. The attention which these scholars of the new thought received from students near and far was intense. Many of the brightest young men from the northern part of the United States felt that their education was incomplete without a year, or two or three, at the feet of some great German intellectual. (The Southerners were too busy repairing the desolation of the Civil War to be able to afford such luxury.) The result for the churches in America was controversy. Far more Christians in this country were repelled than attracted by this new intellectualism. Their efforts to combat this "Modernism," which they firmly believed to be heretical, were to consume vast amounts of energy for years to come.

As early as 1916, Shailer Mathews, then dean of the Divinity

School at the University of Chicago and president that year of the Northern Baptist Convention, admitted to serious "tension within the denomination." Battle lines were beginning to form, and soon the modernist-fundamentalist war was on. The "fundamentalists," as the term implies, held to Christian doctrine as it had been understood throughout the centuries. They were not unmindful of changing times nor were they ignoramuses. The conflict in which they engaged was neither the classic quarrel between town and gown nor the common disagreement between urbanite and peasant. Indeed, numbered among those who extended a call for "A General Conference on Fundamentals" to be held prior to the convention sessions at Buffalo, New York (1920), were five members of the Board of Managers for the Publication Society: George D. Adams, J. W. Brougher, Gove G. Johnson, Luther Keller, and W. B. Riley (president of the Board); also, at least two major employees, H. W. Barras, superintendent of sales, and A. J. Rowland, longtime general secretary. Others among the 155 conveners included leading pastors, such as J. C. Massee, John Roach Straton, W. W. Bustard, John E. Briggs, John B. Champion, S. W. Cummings, Russell H. Conwell, A. C. Dixon, I. N. DePuy, W. T. Elmore, W. B. Hinson, David Lee Jamison, J. A. Maxwell, Cortland Myers, W. H. Rogers, J. F. Rake, John Snape, and J. F. Watson; also some prominent laymen, such as William T. Sheppard, of Lowell, Massachusetts, and M. C. Treat, of Pasadena, California.

Advocates of the liberalism, as it was sometimes called, included the aforementioned Dean Mathews, Harry Emerson Fosdick (who had the backing of John D. Rockefeller, Jr.), Walter Rauschenbusch (who brought the added dimension of his Social Gospel), and many

Walter Rauschenbusch

Baptist seminary professors. Generally speaking, both sides of the controversy were represented by sincere and able men. The Publication Society avoided the controversy insofar as possible. In fact, no discussion of the matter at all appears in the two centennial histories published in 1924 by the Society. A reading of the minutes of Board meetings during the decade of 1914–1924 discloses two oblique references. On May 26, 1920, the Board adopted a publication policy which stated, in part: "Baptists do not think alike. . . . It does not seem Baptistic that the Society should serve one wing of the people to the exclusion of the other. . . ." Thus, as far as the book publishing committee was concerned, there was some recognition of differences in the denomination and a determination to serve both sides. Another possible reference to theological turbulence of the times was an action taken on June 25, 1921, when it was voted to oppose the acceptance of gifts with a creedal limitation contrary to the New Hampshire or Philadelphia Confession of Faith or any other confession of faith which might be adopted by the Convention.

Apparently reacting to the situation, the board in 1922 adopted a directive for its editors and writers of Sunday School materials which should have satisfied most ardent fundamentalists. These tests were:

1. Is he (she) a genuine Christian, intelligent, and spiritual?
2. Does he have a passion for souls?
3. Is he vitally interested in community welfare and service?
4. Does he know and appreciate the educational task of the church?
5. Is he true to our accepted Baptist position—loyal to the Bible, to Christ, to the church, to the denomination, and to the great movements of the kingdom?

Should there have been any doubt where the director of the colporter missionary department stood, Samuel Neil would dispel all questions as he declared that same year, "An empty grave, an empty Cross, mean an occupied Throne . . . He lives, I know He lives."

And so the Publication Society entered the second century of its ministry determined to preach the Word, but not to argue about it!

SOCIAL SERVICE

Another point which was becoming clear as the twentieth century of the Christian church began to unfold was that the dimension of social responsibility must be included in future building of the kingdom. At the May meeting of the Convention in 1912, a resolution was adopted commending to the favorable consideration of the Publication Society the concern of social service. Acting upon this request in September of that year, the Society established the Department of Social Service and Baptist Brotherhood. This was the forerunner of the present organization of American Baptist Men, administratively related to the Board of Educational Ministries, and the department of social action in the Board of National Ministries. In addition there is now a Statements of Concern Committee which prepares statements for consideration at the biennial meeting.

The Publication Society had been responsive to social problems even before 1912. Tracts had been published entitled *Dwight on Drunkenness* and *Intemperance.* In 1829, Noah Davis in his annual report had related the experience of one pastor so moved by the argument of *Dwight on Drunkenness* that he notified his congregation he would no longer offer "ardent spirits" when they visited him and wished none offered him when he visited them! In view of the problems caused by liquor among the clergy of the frontier, as well as among the laity, this must have been a most reasonable request. Other early publications of the Society continued the temperance theme, including *Wisdom's Voice to the Rising Generation on Intemperance, The Sting of the Adder,* and *Joseph Murray, or the Young Prodigal.*

To give leadership to the social service work in the World War I period, Dr. Samuel Zane Batten of Des Moines College was called as secretary and Dr. J. W. Graves of Iowa and Dr. J. Foster Wilcox of Massachusetts as promotion men. Shortly thereafter, in cooperation with the Home Mission Society, another concern was identified and staffed. Dr. Rolvix Harlan, president of Sioux Falls College, South Dakota, was placed in charge of the division of Rural Life and Community.

The problems of beverage alcohol and the limitations of an agricultural society were met through published materials and program staff involvement. Particularly was the liquor business viewed as unalloyed evil. What a victory was claimed when the Eighteenth Amendment passed! Much, much more appears in the official records of the Society about this than about the tribulation of the war "to make the world safe for democracy." The latter was almost totally ignored; temperance was taught in a special lesson once a quarter! In fact, more emphasis was placed on temperance than on all other social issues combined.

At this point, one is pressed to ask questions about other social concerns. What about women's rights? What about race? What about the great immigration from Europe?

With regard to the latter, the responsibility was borne largely by the Home Mission Society. Nevertheless, colporters were appointed by the Publication Society and religious materials, particularly Scriptures, were prepared and printed in many languages. The suffragette movement, however, seemed to have less impact in religious journalism than in either home or foreign missions where in both cases Woman's boards were formed. No Women's American Baptist Publication Society was established. On the contrary, from the first, women supported the general Society through their auxiliaries and other means. At least two women served on the Board of Directors prior to the centennial year of 1924, Mrs. Charles H. Banes and Miss Grace Dickerson. At the same time two department chiefs were women: Miss A. E. Meyers, missionary editor; and Miss Nan F. Weeks, editor of children's publications. Also many women were serving in clerical and secretarial positions.

The factor of race relations was another matter. Although Baptists of the North opposed slavery vigorously and saw the denomination rent at the Mason-Dixon Line rather than send a slaveholder as a foreign missionary, and while they responded splendidly in helping to fill the educational gap among the Blacks at the close of the Civil War with the establishment of educational institutions and the preparation of educational materials, nevertheless the wave of brotherhood broke somewhere on the rocks of reconstructionism. About the time that the "separate but equal" doctrine was being accepted by the U.S. Supreme Court, the American Baptist Publication Society was being forced into a comparable impasse. The Society's materials had been long used by the Negro Baptist churches and most of the education of their leadership, particularly beyond the secondary level, had been obtained in White-sponsored schools. It was natural to expect that Black authorship would soon develop. In response to this situation, Dr. Griffith invited a number of Black leaders to prepare articles for the popular *Sunday School Teacher* magazine. Unfortunately, however, even the powerful Dr. Griffith was not able to stem the tide of public reaction against this plan, and he was forced to withdraw his invitation. The net result of this fiasco was the continued neglect of the issue by the Society and the establishment of the Publishing Board of the National Baptist Convention in 1895.

More positive evidence of concern for Black Baptists is slight. The Reverend H. H. Mitchell was a student for a brief time at Crozer Seminary in 1876, but his opportunities were limited. According to his grandson, the Reverend Dr. Henry H. Mitchell, "he had to eat in the kitchen and sleep out in town." However, time—and Baptists— do change. The grandson in the late 1960s headed the first Black Studies Program at the Colgate Rochester Divinity School, and his wife, Ella, served as a member of the Board of Education and Publication for many years, part of the time as president. In 1902, it was reported that sometime previously a Mrs. Harvey Johnson, a Black pastor's wife from Baltimore, had written two books published by the Publication Society entitled *Clarence and Corinne* and *The Hazeley Family*. Both were adapted for the Sunday school. In 1924, the minutes of the American Baptist Publication Society Board show that a colporter was appointed to work "among the colored people" of the Imperial Valley, California, at the modest annual salary of $900.

It was not a perfect Society which closed its pages on the first hundred years of its history, but it was a good Society. The Publication Society had come of age.

4. Training *the Witnes*

The
Founding
of
Baptist
Educational
Institutions

The union of the two main roots of the current Board of Educational Ministries, i.e., the Publication Society and the Board of Education, brought together two groups that had been cooperating with varying degrees of closeness for a long time. It may be recalled that the origin of the Publication Society lay largely with men connected with Columbian College (now George Washington University). A corresponding two-fold concern for an educated constituency, both clergy and laity, brought into being the Board of Education in 1911. The account of its antecedents, its leadership, and its triumphs and trials is the story of this chapter.

EARLY BAPTIST COLLEGES (Eastern Area)

Prior to the Revolutionary War, American Baptists had established one institution of higher learning—Brown University. Not until after the War of 1812, however, was there sufficient awareness of the need for advanced education to bring other institutions into being. Between that conflict and the Civil War, many other colleges that contine to this day in one form or another were founded.

Brown University, Providence, Rhode Island, arose out of a Baptist academy founded by Isaac Eaton, pastor of the church at

Hopewell, New Jersey. Begun in 1756, the academy functioned for eleven years. The Philadelphia Association had for a long time been concerned about higher education, and finally, under the leadership of Morgan Edwards, pastor of Philadelphia's First Baptist Church, it sent Hopewell's James Manning to Rhode Island to survey the situation. Receiving a favorable welcome, he established Rhode Island College in 1764 at Warren, partway between Providence and Newport. That same year, he organized a Baptist church there, and three years later he helped found the Warren Association, which at one time included most of New England.

In 1770 the college moved to nearby Providence, enticed to do so, no doubt, by an offer of 4280 pounds from the town. The charter strictly forbade religious tests for the students and the faculty was to be open to all "Protestants." The president, however, was to be a Baptist (a requirement deleted in recent years), and the trustees were to include twenty-two Baptists, four Quakers, five Congregationalists, and five Episcopalians.

Among the supporters of the college in Rhode Island were the Brown brothers, sixth-generation descendants of the Reverend Chad Brown, who had been an associate of Roger Williams and a pastor of the Providence church. The Brown family members had prospered greatly and were ready for a cause into which they could pour their accumulated wealth and energy. As pastor of the Providence church, James Manning enlisted their support for the young college. Joseph Brown became a professor, serving without pay. His brother John accepted the chief responsibility of erecting a handsome new meeting house for the church, still used as in its earliest days not only "for the public worship of Almighty God" but "also for holding commencements in." Nicholas Brown, although not a member of the church, supported it and gave the organ for the new building. It was the college, however, that attracted most of his interest and most of his benefactions. Not unmindful, the college in 1804 changed its name to Brown University in his honor.

Today, Brown University is a great academic institution and an active member of that select group known as the "Ivy League." Its relationship to the Baptist cause, however, is strictly historical.

Colby College, chartered by the state of Massachusetts, was given a township of land north of Bangor in 1813, but because of the remoteness of this site a location at Waterville was adopted in its stead. By 1820 a new charter had been granted by the Maine legislature (which had gained jurisdiction with the creation of the state), a small faculty had been appointed, and a student body gathered. The first class consisted of two, including George Dana Boardman, who in his brief lifetime of thirty years was to introduce the Karens of Burma to Christ.

The college takes its name from Gardner Colby, a prosperous Boston merchant and industrialist whose gift of $50,000 proved to be the stimulus that helped bring the school into the front ranks of academic institutions. In 1970, the school enrolled over 1,600 students, listed an endowment of over $14,000,000, and had a property valuation of over $61,000,000. Colby still treasures its Baptist heritage, but no longer maintains any corporate ties with the denomination.

Colgate University and the University of Rochester. Colgate had its beginning in the pioneer days of central New York State. Samuel Payne, of Hamilton, was a devout Baptist and a farmer. Overcome by opportunities given to him by God, after felling the first tree in the forest on the land he was clearing, he knelt there in prayer and consecrated himself and his possessions to God's cause. Sometime after this, twelve other like-minded brethren gathered in a neighbor's house, organized The Baptist Education Society of the State of New York, and took up dues of one dollar each for a treasury. The date was September 24, 1817. Shortly thereafter five students were accepted for instruction by Daniel Hascall, pastor of the Baptist church at Hamilton. Two of the students were Jonathan Wade and Eugenio Kincaid, who later became missionaries to Burma.

The school started by Hascall, Payne, and others was formally opened on May 1, 1820, and served for nineteen years as a seminary for young men preparing for the ministry and the mission field. It was then proposed that enrollment be opened to "a limited number of young men who have not the ministry in view." Alarmed at the intrusion of secularism, the pious objected and so did the politicians. Finally, in 1846, the negotiations and discussions were concluded and the institution was divided into the Hamilton Theological Seminary and Madison University.

As with many a compromise, the settlement of peace only seeded the growth of dissent. By then, western New York State was burgeoning and felt itself to be in the wave of the future. Some at the Hamilton institution agreed and a majority voted to move to Rochester. Others cried, "Foul!" and the matter landed in the courts.

Shurtleff College, Alton, Illinois (closed in 1957)

Richard West and his painting *Indian Christ in Gethsemane,* Bacone College
Chapel

Bacone College, Bacone, Oklahoma

The judgment was that the two schools should remain in Hamilton; but, Baptists being Baptists, a substantial group of faculty and trustees ignored this decision and removed to Rochester. Here, the University of Rochester was established in 1850 and has done very well. Its constantly enlarging campus is valued at many millions of dollars. For years it has been among the leading academic institutions in the country.

So, also, the school at Hamilton has grown. Within three years after the schism, there were more students there than before. Angered to a fervor by the suggestion that Hamilton was being bypassed, its loyal supporters set out to prove the correctness of their judgment. In this they were greatly assisted by James Colgate, of New York City, who had long undergirded the work at Hamilton and in 1891 gave Madison University a million dollars! Thereupon Colgate University was born, and it has gone on to heights equal to that of Rochester. However, neither carries Baptist affiliation any longer.

George Washington University, as we have seen in an earlier chapter, grew out of a small theological school maintained by Dr. William Staughton, pastor of the Sansom Street Baptist Church, Philadelphia. It was moved to Washington, D.C., in 1822 to form the nucleus of Columbian College at the urging of Luther Rice, recently returned from Burma. Strongly convinced of the need for a college in the new capital city, Rice had led the Baptist General Convention at its second meeting in 1817 to adopt the plan, and he had been given the task of bringing the project into being. The college was chartered in 1821.

Few colleges have had such an auspicious beginning—formed by a national religious body, chartered by the federal government, promoted by a dedicated genius, composed of a devout student body, and led by an experienced faculty. Yet matters did not go well. A clash between the college and the school of theology caused the withdrawal of the seminary faculty to Massachusetts, where they formed the Newton Theological Institution. The next year, 1826, the General Convention found the double burden of missions and education too much and abandoned the latter. Dr. Staughton resigned in April, 1829, and died in December of the same year at the home of his son who was on the medical faculty of the school. The college itself closed, but somehow it reopened and struggled along. The rental of its property to the government during the Civil War rescued the school from financial embarrassment, and it gained the solid support of William Corcoran, a partner of G. W. Riggs in the banking business and an Episcopalian by affiliation. In 1903, the name was changed to George Washington University. It is now one of the major educational centers in the Middle Atlantic area. Its graduate schools in law and medicine, which date from the beginning, are especially noted. The university, however, no longer maintains any Baptist affiliation.

Bucknell University, another of the eastern Baptist colleges to be founded prior to the Civil War, was established in Lewisburg, Pennsylvania, and chartered in 1846. The need for a school to educate their children under Christian auspices was keenly felt by the Baptists of central Pennsylvania, and in that year they opened such an institution in the basement of the local Baptist church. For the first five years the acting president was Stephen W. Taylor, who wrote the charter, developed the curriculum, selected the textbooks, prepared the bylaws, laid the foundations for the library, and developed support for the newborn school. Without him, it is said, almost certainly the university would never have existed.

Included in the original board of trustees were three remarkable men whose talents combined to make a forceful and successful team. William Bucknell has been introduced before. The munificent gifts of this stalwart son-in-law of John P. Crozer enabled the school to achieve a stability perhaps not otherwise possible. Also there was Dr. Eugenio Kincaid, one of the first graduates of Hamilton Institute (now Colgate University), famed associate of Adoniram Judson in Burma, and earlier a missionary-pastor in central Pennsylvania. Finally, there was Dr. William Shadrach, a remarkable Welsh preacher who had served as pastor in the state and as executive officer of the Pennsylvania Baptist Convention. For six years he devoted himself to the success of the college at Lewisburg and, seeing a good foundation laid, became, in 1853, corresponding secretary for the American Baptist Publication Society.

Although Bucknell University has had its share of difficulties over the years, it has never experienced the depth of agony many similar schools endured. Currently, the university enrolls approximately three thousand students, has property valued at over twenty million dollars and an endowment of approximately an equal amount. Although it still maintains many informal ties with the denomination, formal ties between the university and the Board of Education and Publication were dissolved by mutual agreement in 1971.

73

Interdenominational Theological
Center, Atlanta, Georgia

Spelman College, Atlanta, Georgia

Danforth Chapel,
Morehouse College, Atlanta,
Georgia

Virginia Union University,
Richmond, Virginia

75

EARLY COLLEGES (Central and Western)

A matter of special concern to the Baptists coming into the raw frontier of the Mississippi Valley in the early 1800s was education, first for ministers and then for the constituency. Out of this concern they founded a number of colleges.

Shurtleff College. John Mason Peck, pioneer Baptist missionary to the West, keenly felt the need for educational institutions and therefore opened a seminary in a building he had constructed on his farm in Illinois, sixteen miles east of St. Louis, Missouri. In so doing he was responding indignantly to the anti-missionary spirit of Southern Illinois Baptists, led by Daniel Parker, which had been extensive enough to lead the Illinois Union Association to censure Peck for his missionary work.

The school was moved to Upper Alton, Illinois, at the suggestion of Jonathan Going, then pastor of the First Baptist Church of Worcester, Massachusetts, who thought the new location to be more strategic. For many years Peck was unable to secure a charter for his school from the Illinois legislature due to the influence of the Primitive (anti-missionary) Baptists. However, the persistent Peck persuaded the citizens of Alton to lend their financial support and convinced the founders of two Baptist academies to merge their schools with his. He thus was enabled to buy 122 acres of land adjoining Upper Alton, and the Alton Seminary was opened with Hubbel Loomis, principal of one of the closed academies, as president. In spite of these victories, times were hard and the school lived a tenuous existence.

Finally, in 1835 Dr. Peck made an extensive journey east attending Baptist conventions of various sorts and pleading the cause of the school in Illinois. He had long conversations with Nicholas Brown, who had contributed so substantially to Brown University, with Lewis Colby of Boston, and with others. Among the latter was Benjamin Shurtleff, a medical doctor of that city. From Dr. Shurtleff the persistent Peck received a gift of $10,000, a sum about equal to the amount raised from other contacts.

With money in hand, the school was chartered by the legislature, but with a stipulation generated by the Primitive Baptists that forbade the establishment of a theological department. The broader judgment eventually prevailed, however, and in 1841 this restriction was removed. Peck and the missionary Baptists had their school. Shurtleff College, as it was then called, continued until 1957, when through difficulties not unlike those of its formative years it was closed. Proceeds of the sale of its property to Southern Illinois State University were used to establish a fund for higher education in Illinois and greater St. Louis. It is administered by the Shurtleff Fund Board, representing regional Baptist interests and the Board of Educational Ministries.

Denison University, Granville, Ohio. For years after Peck's seminary opened, another pioneer school had its beginning. It was an institution destined for strength and increasingly effective service. On May 25, 1830, a group of seventeen men met to establish a literary and theological institution to serve the educational needs of Baptists of the state of Ohio. After spending one full year considering several potential sites, the founders chose Granville in May, 1831. This anniversary meeting was significant also for a broader conception of the proposed institution which developed, largely due to the presence of Jonathan Going of Worcester, Massachusetts, mentioned earlier in connection with Shurtleff College. Going, who later became president of Denison, felt that the aim of the institution as first conceived was too narrow. As a result of his influence the new institution did not have theological education as its dominant concern but placed great emphasis on classical and scientific studies. In 1845 the name of the Granville Literary and Theological Institution was changed to Granville College, and in 1853 was changed again to Denison University due to a pledge of $10,000 from William S. Denison, of Adamsville, Ohio.

Like so many other college histories Denison's story is one of stress and weakness, of devotion and sacrifice, until men of vision and resources provided the means which made possible the development of the institution. It has now become one of the most highly accredited of the church-related colleges of the country. Through the years Denison University has carried on a great tradition of scholarship and religious devotion. In 1970 it had nearly 2,000 students and an endowment of approximately $16,000,000. It is still offically related to the denomination.

Kalamazoo College. Kalamazoo College had its beginning in the vision and devotion of two men, Rev. Thomas W. Merrill and Judge Caleb Eldrid. Merrill had opened a small school in 1830 in Ann Arbor, but his petition for a charter failed—probably because of the requirement that two-thirds of the trustees should be Baptists. Finally, in 1833 after three more failures, a bill passed the legislature

77

incorporating the Michigan and Huron Institute. The next two years were spent in debate on location until in 1835 the village of Bronson, now Kalamazoo, subscribed $2,500 for land and buildings and thus was selected as the site for the school. Instruction began in the fall of 1836. The name was changed to Kalamazoo College in 1855. The early decades of the college were filled with difficulty, including the competition of a branch of the University of Michigan located in Kalamazoo, and the attempt for eighteen years to operate a theological seminary side by side with the college. But beginning in 1892 and during the four decades following, Kalamazoo College emerged from the stage of frontier educational experiment to an assured position of permanence in the educational life of the church, the state, and the nation which it continues to hold. Through the years Kalamazoo College has maintained a vital and meaningful relationship to the denomination.

Franklin College. It was at the close of the organizing session for the Indiana Baptist State Convention, 1833, that a group held a post-convention meeting for the purpose of establishing a college in that area. The next spring fourteen men gathered together to complete the initial action. They were Henry Bradley, Reuben Coffey, Ezra Fisher, Samuel Harding, John Hobart, Moses Jeffries, John Mason, Lewis Morgan, John McCoy, William Reese, John L. Richmond, Nathaniel Richmond, Eliphalet Williams, and J. V. A. Woods. In all they were a remarkable group. Coffey, Fisher, Reese, the Richmond brothers, Wood, and Williams had been among the first band of missionaries sent to Indiana by the newly formed American Baptist Home Mission Society. They had scarcely arrived on the field when they began organizing a state convention and then a college. Ezra Fisher was pastor at first of the Baptist church at Indianapolis, then at Davenport and Muscatine, Iowa, and finally, with Hezekiah Johnson, became one of the first two Baptist missionaries to Oregon. His great grandson was Dr. Kenneth Scott Latourette, noted church historian and professor at Yale University. William Reese became the first full-time agent of the General Association (equivalent to the executive minister of the state convention). Three of his sons became Baptist ministers. Cyrus Williams gained the reputation of having "organized more Baptist churches than any other pastor or missionary on the Pacific coast." Eli served as general agent for the Indiana Baptists and then, after a time in Texas doing educational and evangelistic work, settled in the San Joaquin Valley in California where he spent many years in establishing churches and missions.

In addition to the foregoing notables among the founders of Franklin College was John McCoy, son of Rev. William McCoy, of Fayette County, Pennsylvania, and then of Clark County, Indiana. Although neither John nor his brothers James and Royce ever became as famous as the fourth brother, Isaac, all were ardent champions of the educational and missionary spirit among Baptists and did much to lay solid foundations for the extensive witness in Indiana. Isaac McCoy's work among the American Indians needs no emphasis.

In 1970 the school had an enrollment of nearly 800 students, a property valuation of over $5,000,000, and an endowment of a little less. The college maintains its status as a recognized American Baptist institution, and in 1964 its president, Dr. Harold W. Richardson, became executive secretary of the American Baptist Board of Education and Publication, a position he held until 1973.

William Jewell College. Missouri Baptists, strongly influenced by the educational ideals of John Mason Peck and Luther Rice, began discussing the founding of a Baptist college in 1843 when they received a $10,000 challenge gift from Dr. William Jewell, a physician of Columbia, Missouri. After much difficulty raising the conditional $30,000 required by Dr. Jewell's challenge gift and much debate over location, the college was chartered in 1849 to be located at Liberty, Clay County, Missouri. The early days were not easy, and the institution closed for brief periods in 1852 and 1855. Part of the difficulty was due to the tendency of individual Baptists to start competing colleges. Between 1849 and 1859 there were six Baptist colleges established in Missouri, and between 1869 and 1879 there were seven more. Reopening in 1857, the college weathered the trials of the Civil War and negotiated mergers with two of the competitive colleges that had been established. The progress has continued and the contribution of William Jewell College has multiplied.

William Jewell College is unique in that it is dually related to the Southern Baptist Convention and to the American Baptist Churches. Because of differing philosophies of the two denominations regarding denominational control of college, the present relationship to the American Baptist Churches is ambiguous. Although there was an earlier agreement that presidents would alternate between American and Southern Baptists, the last three presidents of William Jewell have all been Southern Baptists, and the patterns of governance are basically those of a Southern Baptist institution. However, the college has made no effort to sever its historic American Baptist ties.

Linfield College, like most such institutions, has roots in many different places. One of these was in the California gold fields of 1849. The Reverend Ezra Fisher, a founder of Franklin College and a missionary of the American Baptist Home Mission Society to Oregon, suddenly found himself without supplies (the boxes sent out from the East had been lost at sea) and without a congregation (they were busy digging gold in California). Being a practical man, he went where the people were and dug for gold, too. Two months' labor restored his economic situation and he returned to Oregon. Here, however, instead of resting he plunged into the task of curing ignorance. His gold-field money was promptly invested in a donation land claim which he took out with his fellow missionary, Rev. Hezekiah Johnson, and one other. The property was a 600-acre piece on a plateau at the east of the growing town of Oregon City. The new owners at once set aside fifty-one acres for a college and began the organization of the Oregon Baptist Education Society to give broader support to their school, Oregon Baptist College. Meanwhile, members of the Christian denomination at McMinnville, Oregon, were also in the process of establishing a school. They had some land, an unfinished building, a few students, and many headaches. Finally, these two roots—the one at Oregon City and the other at McMinnville—merged into one trunk: a Baptist college. Oregon City supplied the president, Rev. G. C. Chandler, (later) its tangible assets of $1,000, and its bell, which had been specially requested of the American Baptist Home Mission Society.

The college at McMinnville lived from hand-to-mouth for years. Periodically, it would be rescued by some sacrifice, as the assumption of "fostering care over the institution" by the Central Association of Baptist Churches; or the election of the Reverend Dr. Leonard W. Riley, secretary of the state convention, as president. Dr. J. Whitcomb Brougher, a member of the trustees and later president of the Northern Baptist Convention, made the motion in 1906 to invite Dr. Riley to become president and "to pull it [the college] out of the hole if he can." With the help of a fortune amassed by the widow of a clergyman, Mrs. George F. Linfield, and a substantial gift by a layman from California, M. C. Treat, this is precisely what Dr. Riley did. Mrs. Linfield must be regarded as a financial wizard, for on her salary as a school teacher and on that of her husband as a minister, she had by the 1920s gathered an estate worth about $300,000. This all came to the college which became known as Linfield. With Mr. Treat's gift of $383,000, the college was now on a firm foundation.

Today, Linfield enrolls about 1,200 students, has a beautiful campus valued at $6,000,000 and an endowment of half as much. It maintains affiliation with the American Baptist Churches and regularly sends some of its graduates into church-related vocations and into service in the local churches.

Sioux Falls College. As early as 1872 the Southern Dakota Baptist Association with only nine churches and a total of 157 members voted to take immediate steps for the establishment of an educational institution. Because of an inadequate supporting constituency, crop failures, and other financial problems, the school did not open until 1883, when classes were held in the basement of the First Baptist Church of Sioux Falls. The first building was begun in 1884, but progress of the college was slow, and the first college graduate did not receive a diploma till 1904. Throughout its history the school has been hampered by lack of a strong supporting constituency and in the early years by the presence of competing institutions in adjacent states. In spite of all its difficulties, however, dedicated friends and committed alumni have remained faithful. The college regained its accreditation in 1958, and during the sixties rose to its greatest eminence due in large part to the support of two dedicated Baptist laymen, Dr. Joseph E. Salsbury, of Iowa, and Mr. Norman B. Mears, of Minnesota.

In 1929 the records of Des Moines University were transferred to Sioux Falls when that college closed. The demise of Des Moines University is itself a tragic story of competitiveness and lack of overall educational policy in the state of Iowa, where three American Baptist institutions at Burlington, Des Moines, and Pella could not agree in time on a unified program that would create one strong institution. Burlington College closed and its records were transferred to Des Moines. Central College, Pella, could no longer survive and sold its campus and its name to the Dutch Reformed Church in 1919. The proceeds of the sale were merged with the assets of Des Moines College, and a new institution known as Des Moines University was established. However, too much history had passed and the university could not survive the beginning of the depression in 1929. Another midwestern victim of the depression was Grand Island College, Grand Island, Nebraska, which closed its doors in 1931 and

Florida Memorial College, Miami, Florida

merged with Sioux Falls College in Sioux Falls, thus leaving Sioux Falls as the only American Baptist institution in the five-state area. It remains actively related to the American Baptist Churches.

Ottawa University. In 1860 when the Kansas Baptist Convention was organized, the Kansas Baptists voted to establish Roger Williams University. Through the influence of John Tecumseh Tauy Jones, an Ottawa Indian, negotiations were conducted whereby the Ottawas agreed to give to the university twenty thousand acres of land, and in return the trustees agreed to board, clothe, and educate a number not exceeding fifty of the Ottawa children every year for thirty years. At the end of that period the Ottawas were to be entitled to ten scholarships in the university forever. In recognition of this commitment to the education of Indians, the university was renamed Ottawa University in 1865, the year of its incorporation.

Instruction began in a rented building the following year with forty Indian students enrolled. However, in the manner of dealing with the American Indian typical of the government in the latter half of the nineteenth century, Congress in 1872 passed a bill calling for the forfeiture of the Indian lands granted to the university and a commission was sent to Ottawa demanding the university property. The act was protested by all parties, including the American Baptist Home Mission Society, and in March, 1873, Congress repealed the act and established a commission to ascertain and determine the equitable interest of the contending parties. The final settlement with the Indians may be summarized as follows:

1. The college got 640 acres of land where the buildings were located at Ottawa, Kansas.
2. 1280 acres were to be selected from the unsold lands of the 20,000 set apart in the Treaty of 1862.
3. All but one Indian on the college board of trustees were asked to resign.
4. All obligations to the Indians would forever cease.
5. All notes and mortgages held by the trustees were to be turned over to the Indians.
6. The Indians were to get the rest of their land back.

The action significantly changed the direction of the institution. There followed decades of great difficulty including financial stress, fire, and agitation for moving of the institution to another locality, all of which retarded progress.

Following the turn of the century, however, Ottawa University was well on its way to recognition as a strong educational institution. Very early in its history it had developed strong ties with the Kansas Baptist Convention, and in the 1930s it developed a pattern of financing unique among American Baptist collegiate institutions. Known as the Kansas Plan, it provides for a percentage return of all missionary dollars raised in Kansas Baptist churches to go to the university. At the present time under the presidency of Dr. Peter Armacost (who was also elected president of the American Baptist Churches as of January, 1974), Ottawa University has developed a creative educational program that is attracting considerable attention in academic circles.

Alderson-Broaddus College. West Virginia gives a striking example of what has occurred all too often in American Baptist educational history. Dr. Richard E. Shearer, currently the president of Alderson-Broaddus College, once wrote, "Baptists have been more zealous than wise in their educational pursuits in West Virginia. As a religious group they have been quick to see the need of educational institutions, but often slow to see the implications of their visions." As a result, institutions were established which had little chance of survival, and out of five schools established by West Virginia Baptists, three no longer exist and the other two are united in one institution.

The three short-lived institutions were Rector College, founded in 1838 at Pruntytown; Allegheny College, established at Blue Sulphur Springs in 1859; and Shelton College, opened in 1872 at St. Albans. The two institutions which merged to form the present college were Broaddus College and Alderson Academy and Junior College. Broaddus began as a girls' school in 1871 in Winchester, Virginia, and was then known as the Winchester Female Institute. In 1876 it was moved to Clarksburg, West Virginia, as the Broaddus Female College. In 1888 the college became coeducational, and a few years later the name was changed to the Broaddus Classical and Scientific Institute. In 1906 the college moved to Philippi as the Broaddus Institute. In 1918 the name was changed to Broaddus College, and seven years later it became a regular four-year liberal arts college.

Alderson Academy had been established in the southern section of the state in 1901, largely through the efforts of Miss Emma Alderson, the daughter of the last surviving trustee of Allegheny College. For the first decade it was largely an enterprise of the Alderson family until the school was taken under the sponsorship of the West Virginia Baptist Convention in 1911.

With the coming of the depression in the thirties, both institutions faced severe financial crisis. The state convention itself assumed an active role in the situation, assuming responsibility for the debts of the two institutions, and affirmed a policy lending to the establishment of one Baptist college for West Virginia. In 1932 a new charter was obtained bringing about Alderson-Broaddus College located on the former Broaddus campus at Philippi. However, financial difficulties continued to plague the college and at times threatened its very existence. Following World War II and especially with the coming of President Shearer in 1949, Alderson-Broaddus made remarkable strides, presently having a reputation as one of the outstanding private colleges of Appalachia. The presence of Broaddus Hospital on the campus of the college has led to the development of significant paramedical programs including the first four-year physician's assistant program in any private college in America. In 1970 it enrolled about 1,100 students. It has an annual operating budget of approximately $3,000,000 and continues to maintain a very strong denominational relationship.

Colorado Women's College. Although the Board of the Colorado Woman's College Society was incorporated by the legislature of Colorado in 1888 and a cornerstone for a new building for the college was laid at Denver in 1890, the college did not open its doors to students until September, 1909. From the beginning it was dedicated to the education of women against the opposition of some forces in the state who wanted to see the institution be coeducational. In 1916 the college was reorganized as a Junior College. As such it continued to progress. It survived the depression of the thirties and rose to new heights following World War II. It became a four-year degree-granting institution in the 1960s.

During that same decade supporters of Colorado Woman's College were encouraged by a gift by a Denver businessman reputed to be valued at $25,000,000. In appreciation the college honored the donor by changing the name of the college to Temple Buell College. However, the gift, which was in the form of real estate, was tied up with certain provisions which prevented the college from receiving any income for the first seven years and then allowed it to receive only small amounts in succeeding years. In the meantime, other friends and donors, believing the college to be enjoying the income from the

$25,000,000 gift, withheld some of their normal support. The result was a severe financial crisis for the college. In 1973 the college repudiated the gift and changed the name to Colorado Women's College (changing from Woman's to Women's). It remains one of the fine institutions for women in the United States.

University of Redlands. After an abortive attempt to establish an educational institution in Southern California with the chartering of Los Angeles University in 1888, Southern California Baptists established the University of Redlands in 1909 in the city of Redlands. Four years after its opening, a visitor to the institution wrote, "The University of Redlands is one of the surprises of the educational world." Almost spontaneously it sprang into being as a full-fledged institution of learning. Although experiencing severe financial difficulties in its first five years, by 1920 it had reached a position of financial stability and was able to move through the subsequent decades in the front rank of liberal arts colleges in the nation. In the late sixties, rather than expand the size of the university, it elected to achieve growth by means of cluster colleges, the first being the highly experimental Johnston College, which has gained worldwide recognition. The University of Redlands continues to maintain strong denominational ties.

Free Will Baptist Colleges. In 1911 when the then Northern Baptist Convention merged with the Free Will Baptist Association, three educational institutions with long and distinguished records were added to the list of institutions related to American Baptists. These were Hillsdale College, in Michigan, Bates College, in Maine, and Keuka College, in New York. Of the three institutions, only Keuka, a college for women, remains related to the American Baptist Churches.

Home Mission Society Schools for Minorities. Among the most significant educational institutions making up the American Baptist family were those established by the American Baptist Home Mission Societies, including fifteen for Blacks and one for American Indians. In the period following the Civil War the plight of the freedman awakened widespread concern throughout the northern states and the response was immediate and generous. In 1865, a few weeks after the close of the Civil War, a new era opened in the work of the American Baptist Home Mission Society as it sought to contribute to the enlarged life opening before freedmen. By 1869 seven schools were in existence. Virginia Union University, Richmond, Virginia, resulted from the merging of two institutions from this early group, namely Wayland Seminary, Washington, D.C., and Richmond Theological Seminary. Later a school for women, Hartshorn Memorial College, united with the university. Shaw University, Raleigh, North Carolina, was opened in 1865 and has developed into one of the strongest of the Black institutions of higher learning. Morehouse College traces its origins to the efforts of a Black man, Richard C. Coulter, who opened a branch of the Washington Institute in Augusta in February, 1867. With assistance from the American Baptist Home Mission Society, the institute moved in 1879 to Atlanta under the name Atlanta Baptist Seminary. Still later the name was changed to Morehouse College, and it has grown to be one of the significant institutions for Blacks in America. Morehouse College and its distinguished president, Dr. Benjamin F. Mays, gave leadership to the strengthening of the Atlanta University Center and the Interdenominational Theological Center. Other colleges established were Spelman College, Atlanta, Georgia; Benedict College, Columbia, South Carolina; Leland College, Baker, Louisiana; Bishop College, Marshall, Texas; Storer College, Harper's Ferry, West Virginia; Jackson College, Jackson, Mississippi; two institutions in Florida which were later to become Florida Memorial College of St. Augustine; Roger Williams College, Nashville, Tennessee; Selma College, Selma, Alabama; Arkansas Baptist College, Little Rock, Arkansas; and Mather School, Beaufort, South Carolina.

On October 1, 1935, the relationship of the schools which were then related to the American Baptist Home Mission Society was transferred to the Board of Education. At the time of the transfer the schools coming under the Board of Education numbered eleven: Virginia Union, Storer, Shaw, Benedict, Morehouse, Spelman, Jackson, Leland, Bishop, Florida Normal and Industrial, and Mather. In 1954, with the famous Supreme Court decision, there was an increasing feeling among many whites that Black institutions had outlived their usefulness and that Blacks would now receive their education in white institutions. However, such Black Baptist leaders as Dr. Mays and Dr. Milton F. Curry convinced church leadership in the late fifties and early sixties that such was not the case. The Black institutions had an even more significant role in the years ahead.

The Board of Education was convinced that these institutions had to be strengthened, and certain significant steps were taken toward

Joseph Bond Chapel, University of Chicago

Spanish American Baptist
Seminary, Los Angeles, California

over Newton Theological
ol, Newton Centre,
sachusetts

89

this end. Institutions not capable of surviving were closed, such as Leland College. Others were merged with stronger institutions: Mather with Benedict, and Storer with Virginia Union. Two were relocated from small communities to significant urban areas: Bishop College from Marshall, Texas, to Dallas; Florida Memorial from St. Augustine to Miami. At the present time seven of those eleven institutions remain. All are fully accredited. All are located in significant urban centers in the south. Spelman has recently declared itself to be an independent institution. The remaining six, Benedict, Bishop, Florida Memorial, Morehouse, Shaw, and Virginia Union, continue to maintain strong denominational relationships with American Baptists. They are among the foremost Black institutions in America as exemplified by the fact that five have recently received significant grants from the Ford Foundation.

One of the educational projects of American Baptists which has made a far-reaching contribution to a great people began its service under the name of Indian University in 1880. In 1885 the college moved from Tahlequah to land outside Muskogee, Oklahoma, which was a grant of the Creek nation to the college. The first president was Dr. Almon C. Bacone, for whom the college was named following his death in 1896. Administrative responsibility for Bacone College, a fully accredited junior college, was transferred to the Board of Education in 1970.

Specialized Institutions for Women. Special mention should be made of two institutions which have long years of service to American Baptists in a specialized field. In response to a need for a training school for women missionaries, the Baptist Missionary Training School was opened in Chicago in 1881. It was the first such institution established for the specific education of women for missionary service in succeeding decades. The academic standards were raised and the curriculum was enriched; and by 1936 the program included a full four-year college course leading to B.A. and B.R.E. degrees. By 1961 the educational requirements for women preparing for church vocations had changed so that it was held that such training could more appropriately be given at the graduate level. Therefore, merger negotiations were entered into between BMTS and Colgate Rochester Divinity School and the assets of the sale of property in Chicago were used to endow a women's program at the Divinity School.

Another institution with a similar purpose was the Baptist Institute

for Christian Workers in Philadelphia, founded in 1892 by a former Burma missionary, Ellen H. Cushing. After several decades of training for church vocations, the institution moved in 1952 to Bryn Mawr, Pennsylvania, and in October, 1959, it was approved by the Pennsylvania Department of Instruction as a junior college. In 1965 the name of the institution was changed to Ellen Cushing Junior College with a very specialized program for young women whose academic achievements in high school were in the middle range. Their avowed mission is to help the middle-range student "learn how to learn." A significant number of recent graduates have gone on to successful careers in four-year colleges.

OTHER INSTITUTIONS

Space does not permit us to explore in depth other institutions founded by Baptists, such as Vassar College, Poughkeepsie, New York; Temple University, Philadelphia, Pennsylvania; Keystone Junior College, LaPlume, Pennsylvania; and the University of Chicago. Nor can we more than mention other institutions whose existences were very short-lived, such as Colfax College, Colfax, Washington; University of Seattle and Adelphia College in Seattle; and Ewing College, Ewing, Illinois. In all, over ninety colleges and universities have been established by Baptists in their history. However, as President Shearer said above about West Virginia Baptists, "We have often been more zealous than wise in our educational pursuits."

THEOLOGICAL SEMINARIES

The story of nineteenth-century American Baptist theological seminaries is found intertwined in the account of the birth and growth of the colleges. Basic elements in the various institutions were the same: the desire for an educated clergy, the founding of a school to meet that need, the sacrifice of dedicated supporters, the division of interest between liberal arts and theology, the greater support for the former, and the eventual breaking away of the theological school to form a separate institution. However, there is sufficient difference in the various stories to warrant separate treatment.

Andover Newton Theological School. Newton Theological Institution began, as we have seen, with a group of divinity students taught by Dr. Staughton, pastor of the Sansom Street Church in Philadelphia, and continued briefly in Washington under the umbrella of Columbian College. It found its identity, however, under the leadership of Ira Chase, who guided its relocation to Newton Centre, Massachusetts, where on November 28, 1825, it opened with Chase as first professor.

Massachusetts Baptists were ready for the new school. Gifts were solicited, through which four young men were placed under the instruction of Jeremiah Chaplin, pastor at Danvers. Upon Chaplin's removal to Waterville, Maine, to assume the presidency of the new college there (Colby), his students followed. Massachusetts Baptists persevered, however, in their efforts to establish a viable theological school, urged on by Jonathan Going, who held that a training school for ministers should be quite separate from the liberal arts college. He urged that it was essential for ministerial students to have close contact with proven men of God "to form manners, habits and character." Accepting this thesis, certain Baptist leaders revitalized the school. They were: Lucius Bolles, pastor of the First Baptist Church of Salem and an early supporter of Judson and foreign missions; Jonathan Going, pastor at Worcester and a founder of the American Baptist Home Mission Society; Joseph Grafton, pastor of the Baptist church in Newton for nearly fifty years; Henry Jackson, a protege of Stephen Gano and pastor of the church at Charlestown; Bela Jacobs; Ebenezer Nelson, pastor at Lynn and fund raiser for the new seminary; Daniel Sharp, pastor of the Charles Street Church of Boston for forty-one years and president of the board of the General Convention; and Francis Wayland, pastor of Boston's First Baptist Church and later president of Brown University.

After more than a century of service to the denomination, the institution united with Andover Theological Seminary, a trinitarian Congregational school that had been frustrated in its attempt to merge with unitarian Harvard. Today, Andover Newton stands on the high hill of the Peck estate purchased in 1825 for $4,250. The value of the property 145 years later is over $4,000,000. The endowment is about $9,000,000 and the enrollment exceeds 350 students.

Colgate Rochester/Bexley Hall/Crozer. The divinity school at Rochester, New York, represents, it might be said, the acme of ecumenism. It is known as Colgate Rochester/Bexley Hall/Crozer. Three of the four units are Baptist; Bexley Hall is Episcopalian. President Arthur McKay, who headed the school in the early 1970s, was a Presbyterian. Close relationship is maintained with a Roman

Catholic seminary and with the University of Rochester. When the University of Rochester and its seminary were established as the outgrowth of a dispute with the University at Hamilton (presently Colgate), the traveling time between Rochester and Hamilton was considerable, and both seminaries were needed. At first the college and the seminary at Rochester shared the same building and had a common library. In 1850, when the work began in Rochester, $140,000 was subscribed for the dual institution, but of this sum only about $1,000 was designated for the seminary. The latter institution had a real struggle for survival, but survive it did and independently.

One of the early unique features of the Rochester seminary was the establishment in 1854 of a German department. This not only served a great need by furnishing the rapidly growing German population of nineteenth-century America with Baptist pastoral leadership, but it also brought into the Rochester orbit the Rauschenbusch family—father and son—the scholarly father to head the German department for many years and the activist son, Walter, to reinterpret the gospel emphasizing its social dimensions. The seminary also attracted to its fold members of the Strong family—Augustus, the towering Baptist theologian and president of the school, and Henry, the layman who brought his dedicated money. Other laymen who gave generously over the years were John B. Trevor, of Yonkers, New York, and John J. Jones. John D. Rockefeller was most helpful also. His first substantial gift provided a commodious classroom building with library and chapel (old campus, 1879), and one of his last gifts was the sum of $1,250,000 to aid the unification with the seminary from Colgate University in 1928.

Colgate Divinity School had maintained its independent existence since the separation of Rochester in the mid-nineteenth century. Like Rochester, it had provided significant leadership for American ethnics, Colgate's contribution being an Italian department founded in Brooklyn, New York, under the leadership of Antonio Mangano.

With merger, there has also come separation. The German department became an independent school in 1935 and, as the North American Baptist Seminary, moved to Sioux Falls, South Dakota, in 1949. Colgate Rochester in 1970 had property valued at $2,500,000 and an endowment of $13,000,000. Students enrolled numbered 125.

Crozer Theological Seminary, the newest member of the Rochester family, owes its origin and continuance quite markedly to one family—that of John P. Crozer. Long interested in education, Mr.

Crozer Theological Seminary,
Chester, Pennsylvania, before
relocation

Colgate Rochester/Bexley
Hall/Crozer, Rochester, New York

American Baptist Seminary of
the West, Berkeley, California

Central Baptist Theological
Seminary, Kansas City, Kansas

95

Crozer had given some land for that purpose in Upland, Pennsylvania, and erected a building upon it just before the Civil War. Shortly thereafter the war came, and the building was used for several years as a hospital. After the war and upon the death of the elder Crozer, the family determined to memorialize his memory with the establishment of a training school for ministers. By bringing together the theological department from the university at Lewisburg, the campus at Upland, and an original gift from the heirs of John P. Crozer of a fund of $275,000, the seminary was enabled to be chartered on good foundations in 1867. Samuel, the oldest son, served as president of the trustees for forty-three years. Henry G. Weston, a native of Lynn, Massachusetts, a pastor in Peoria, Illinois, and then in New York City, became president of the new school and remained in that post for forty-one years. To these two Christian men, Baptists owe a great debt.

In 1969, Crozer Seminary enrolled 117 students, held property valued at over $2,500,000, and had $3,168,000 of endowment. The pressure of maintaining a separate theological school and the inducements of the ecumenical environment, however, combined to cause the seminary to unite with Colgate Rochester and Bexley Hall in Rochester, New York, in 1970.

Central Baptist Theological Seminary. Kansas City Baptist Theological Seminary, as the school was known for many years, began in the traditional desire of Baptist people for an educated ministry. While some felt that this need could be met by strengthening the theological department of William Jewell College at Liberty, Missouri, and while others were concerned for strengthening Ottawa University at Ottawa, Kansas, and feared spreading support too thinly, still others argued stoutly for a separate theological school. The latter group, mainly Kansas people, at last prevailed and on August 17, 1901, formally organized the school under the direction of E. B. Meredith, executive secretary of the state convention. Present, in addition to Dr. Meredith, were: F. L. Streeter, F. C. Bingham, W. C. Stiver, James F. Wells, all Kansas pastors; editors S. M. Brown and B. W. Wiseman; and Charles Lovelace, a wealthy layman from Turner, Kansas. Not present, but favorably inclined and long identified with the work were Dr. I. N. Clark, area representative of the American Baptist foreign mission enterprise and later president of the seminary's board for many years; and Dr. Stephen A. Northrop of the First Baptist Church, Kansas City, Missouri.

At first, the seminary served more as a training school for ministerial students without a college background than as a graduate school. Some supporters even suggested that this be its unique task. Others, however, opted for a full-fledged graduate theological institution. The first president was Dr. Philip W. Crannell, pastor of the First Church, Topeka, who for twenty-five years rendered outstanding leadership to church and seminary. Under his guidance a full faculty was gathered, a new campus was obtained, and as the theological dust storms began to arise in the 1920s, the school was given its direction. Said Dr. Crannell, "Our doctrine is sturdily conservative." The seminary affirmed the New Hampshire Confession of Faith "not as an authoritative creed or a perfect expression of divine truth, but as a cautious, moderate, and in all essentials, satisfactory statement of the doctrines commonly received among Baptists, with the understanding on the part of each [professor or trustee] that should he find himself out of harmony with it he will relinquish his position."

Until 1956, Central Baptist Seminary held a relationship with both American and Southern Baptist Conventions. During that year, however, the Board voted sole affiliation with the American Baptists. In 1970 the school listed an enrollment of forty-six, with a property valuation of $1,500,000 and an endowment of over $1,000,000.

The American Baptist Seminary of the West. In common with Baptists elsewhere, California Baptists early recognized the need for an educated ministry. In fact, an educational society for that purpose was organized the same year as the state convention was established, 1853. Progress was slow, however, in spite of numerous efforts. In 1870 the Pacific Association meeting in Santa Rosa purchased the property of the Methodist College in Vacaville, recruited for support, elected a board of trustees, appointed a president, and obtained a charter from the state. In spite of noble efforts by a succession of presidents—Mark Bailey, A. S. Worrell, T. W. Greene, S. A. Taft, and Uriah Gregory—the school did not prosper. In 1883 the institution was moved to Oakland where the rough times continued.

Meanwhile, other efforts more particularly devoted to theological education were underway. It was in 1889 that Dr. C. H. Hobart, pastor of the First Church, Oakland, sponsored a meeting for the purpose of founding such a school. The gathering, composed of representatives from twenty-five churches in California and one from British Columbia, met in Sacramento. The decision to proceed was made; the support of the state convention was sought and granted; a home for the school was found in the First Church, Oakland; the formal opening was set for September, 1890; and a president was selected, Dr. E. H. Gray. Born in Bridgeport, Vermont, and educated at Colby College, Dr. Gray had been chaplain of the U.S. Senate.

The argument for the need of a training school for ministers in the Far West was patent. Here was a vast territory, in size 1,200 miles from north to south and over 1,500 miles west to east, with a burgeoning population and no Baptist seminary. Substantial support, however, did not become as evident as the need. There were times when the school closed, but better days finally came. Dr. Claiborne Hill, pastor of the Tenth Avenue Church, Oakland, was elected president in 1904 and served thirty-three years. Under his leadership the college (originated at Vacaville) was merged with the seminary; a fine campus was built in Berkeley, near the University of California; the approval of ten state conventions in the West was obtained; and a standard theological curriculum was developed. This was the Berkeley Baptist Divinity School.

As the storm clouds of the fundamentalist-modernist war began to form, Dr. Hill published a brief statement called "Our Baptist Position" and included in it material on the trinity, the virgin birth, the atonement on the cross, the resurrection, and the return of Christ. While there appears to be no record that this statement was ever officially endorsed by the trustees, it was used by presidents in discussion with new faculty members, and it was spread widely among the churches.

In 1968 the Berkeley school was merged with its southern neighbor, California Baptist Theological Seminary (see chapter 5) to form the American Baptist Seminary of the West, occupying two campuses. At the present time the Seminary of the West is exploring new educational possibilities which would involve only one main campus with several decentralized educational centers.

THE BOARD OF EDUCATION

Following the foregoing stories of courage and sacrifice, of independent action and collective need, there arose what became in 1912 the Board of Education of the Northern Baptist Convention. Long before that year, however, many state boards of education had been established by Baptists, and many earnest attempts had been made to do the same thing on a national scale.

98

One of the first to propose a Baptist educational society on a coast-to-coast base was Dr. Sewell S. Cutting, of the University of Rochester. It was on the occasion of the annual sessions of the New York State convention meeting in Poughkeepsie, 1867. His argument was that the educational societies then were focusing most of their attention upon ministerial training to the neglect of liberal arts, with the result that neither prospered. Later in the year, stimulated by this plea, a committee met in New York City and organized the Baptist Educational Commission. It was agreed to commence operations on January 1, 1868, to gather a broadly based representation, and to dissolve in four years if nothing was accomplished. With this "self-destruct" principle firmly established, the committee set about its task.

Within two years, a general convention of people interested in Christian higher education among Baptists was called. Leading the conveners was Dr. Cutting, supported by Samuel Colgate. Others were the presidents of Brown, Rochester, Colgate, Columbian, and Bucknell universities and Newton and Crozer seminaries. In response to the invitation, there assembled at the Pierrepont Street Church in Brooklyn a glittering array of notables from forty-eight Baptist schools and educational societies. In addition to the institutions just named, the seminary presidents of Hamilton (Colgate), Southern Baptist, and Baptist Union (now the Divinity School of the University of Chicago) and the college presidents of Colby, Vassar, William Jewell, Shurtleff, Chicago, Denison, and Kalamazoo participated. Much enthusiasm was expressed, but complaints were voiced about doing educational work in "detached portions." A decision was made to have three advisory committees: one to meet in Boston, one in Chicago, and one in Richmond. And the word "American" was prefaced to the commission's name, making it the American Baptist Educational Commission.

Two years later, the group met in Philadelphia, where the enthusiasm and attendance were even greater. It was decided to publish a professional journal and to set about raising funds for the schools, but the panic of 1873 and the removal of Dr. Cutting to the American Baptist Home Mission Society effectively stopped both efforts, and the movement died.

Fifteen years later under the inspiration of Dr. Henry L. Morehouse of the American Baptist Home Mission Society, a resurrection took place. Moved by the need of the colleges, particularly in the West, he suggested at the May meetings in Minneapolis that a new Society be organized on a par with the other societies of Northern Baptists, giving real thrust to the needs and direction of higher education.

This attempt reached fruition in Washington, D.C., May 17, 1888, with the founding of the American Baptist Educational Society. The president was Francis Wayland III, son of the famous president of Brown University and himself the distinguished dean of Yale Law School. First vice-president was Lewis B. Ely, of Carrolton, Missouri, a prominent merchant and a trustee and financial agent for William Jewell College. Second vice-president was George Pillsbury, of Minnesota. The secretary was Lansing Burrows, Jr., pastor of First Baptist, Augusta, Georgia, and record secretary for thirty-three years of the Southern Baptist Convention. Treasurer was Joshua Levering, prominent philanthropist of Baltimore, Maryland, president of the board of trustees of Southern Baptist Seminary for forty years and president of the Southern Baptist Convention for three years.

On the executive board were such men as Henry L. Morehouse, of the American Baptist Home Mission Society; William R. Harper, later president of the University of Chicago; William H. Doane, talented composer and prosperous manufacturer; Samuel Colgate, New York businessman and patron of Colgate University; George Dana Boardman, son of the famous missionary, long-time pastor of Philadelphia's First Baptist Church, and trustee of the University of Pennsylvania; John B. Stetson, of Philadelphia, noted manufacturer of hats; and A. C. Dixon, then of Baltimore and later to be pastor of the Moody Church in Chicago and of Spurgeon's Tabernacle in London. Two others especially active in the work were Rev. Frederick T. Gates, pastor of the Central Baptist Church, Minneapolis, who became the corresponding secretary, and oil magnate John D. Rockefeller.

Certainly the people involved had both the means and the motivation to make the work succeed. Mr. Rockefeller supplied most of the funds and much of the interest. The latter point is remarkable, for at first he evidenced limited concern. In a letter dated August 6, 1888, i.e., three months after the organizational meeting of the new society, he admitted to Dr. Morehouse that he was not convinced of the project. Perhaps, he continued, it was because "of a lack of sufficient information." If that were the case, the proper information began to reach him, for six months later he made an offer of $100,000, and other larger gifts came along in prompt succession.

It was the intention of the Educational Society not to found institutions, but to offer supplemental help and guidance. In accordance with this policy, "deed money" was appropriated. Some of the institutions so aided between May, 1889, and July, 1891, were Cook Academy, Havana, New York ($16,000); the University at Jackson, Tennessee ($13,000); Kalamazoo ($15,000); Ottawa ($10,000); Carson Newman ($6,200); Franklin ($10,000); Mercer ($10,000). In addition, $1,200,000 was set aside for the reestablishment of the University of Chicago. (The first school of that name had begun in 1856 with leadership from the First Baptist Church and money from Senator Stephen A. Douglas, but it had died in 1886.)

It was not long before Mr. Rockefeller began to have, if not a change of heart, at least a change in direction. He was, according to some, the richest man in the world. His empire founded on oil had grown fantastically, and, as with most very successful men, he had attracted a large and outspoken group of enemies. Lampoonists found him an inviting target. As an earnest follower of the Christian faith in his personal life, he must have found this bitter medicine. Nevertheless, his benevolences to American Baptist work were outstanding. He called the Rev. F. T. Gates in 1893 from his position as secretary of the American Baptist Education Society to counsel in the distribution of the Rockefeller millions. Out of this relationship grew the General Education Board, headed by Gates and funded largely by Rockefeller with gifts through 1927 of some $50,000,000. By this time, the University of Chicago had received $23,000,000.

Long before this time, the Baptist Education Society was defunct. The reliance upon a single individual was not the only reason for its passing, but it was doubtless one of the factors. Another was the constant tension between the ideal and the practical, both in the society itself and in the institutions with which it was concerned. In a report to the society, for instance, a committee studying Columbian University stated: "It thus appears that the denominational control of the University for the present is assured." This judgment was made on the basis that nineteen of the twenty-five overseers and trustees were Baptists. Yet there was no provision or guarantee that this was to continue so. Not long after this prediction, the school became George Washington University and its "denominational control" a dim memory.

Burdened by the continued need of support for struggling schools and for wise counsel for all schools, thoughtful Baptists persisted in their efforts to establish some denominationally based group that would give direction and aid. Among those concerned was Rev. Frank W. Padelford. During the early years of the twentieth century he had been pastor of the Portland Street Church, Haverhill, Massachusetts, and then of the Washington Street Church in Lynn. By 1908 he had become secretary of the Massachusetts Baptist Missionary Society and an advocate of denominational planning in Christian higher education. He was able—a Phi Beta Kappa graduate of Colby College. He was righteous—the son of a minister and a stout opponent of the use of tobacco. Once on a trip to New York City he found lying in the gutter a string of beads, which he picked up and took home to his wife. When a jeweler appraised them for her at $25,000, Padelford again pocketed the jewelry, returned to New York, and searched until he found the owner!

To such a man American Baptists turned when in 1912 at the Convention sessions in Des Moines they made another try at establishing a national board of education. This time they added a feature found to be helpful to other branches of denominational life—corporate membership of the entire registration of convention delegates. This made the Board of Education a full-fledged member of the family and a responsibility of all. The first action of the new board was to search for a leader, and the selection fell upon Dr. Padelford. He was to remain in the post until the coming of Luther Wesley Smith and the union with the Publication Society nearly thirty years later.

Dr. Padelford was not long in moving in upon the situation. First of all he visited the various Baptist-related schools to establish rapport. Then he took a survey. He found, as many had suspected, that Baptists were low on the scale in ratio of college students to church membership. The Presbyterians and the Congregationalists had three times as many students per church member as did the Baptists. Furthermore. using graduate school criteria, only four Baptist colleges rated first class. In other words, Baptists were not attending college in as great numbers proportionately as others, and the schools they were attending were not as strong academically as others.

The solution for this problem was sought in money. More adequate endowments would allow the employment of more adequate faculties, the development of more adequate programs, and the erection of more adequate facilities. So, at the Boston Convention in 1914 was launched the "greatest forward movement ever undertaken by the denomination." The goal was set in the millions of dollars. Then came World War I! Needless to say, the disruption did not help the movement. However, $16,000,000 was raised. Had this amount been spread evenly, the impact would have been greater, but two-thirds of the total was designated for the University of Chicago.

In spite of these limitations, the Board of Education felt encouraged and proceeded to enter other areas of activity. Fundraising services to the institutions were expanded. Guides for the upgrading of curriculum were prepared. Suggestions for the safeguarding of investments were offered. Techniques for recruiting students were developed. Relations with the state and area accrediting agencies were reviewed and strengthened. Then, in addition to these measures directed toward the schools and colleges, other steps were taken toward answering needs of the students. College chaplains were appointed. Baptist pastors located near campuses were aided in their ministry to the students. In some cases buildings were erected or procured as religious activity centers. As momentum increased, so did the scope. The Board began to envisage its area of concern as including the local church. It established a department of Youth Work. Its department of Missionary Education became most effective. The work for girls under the World Wide Guild, led by Alma and Mary Noble, was adopted by thousands of churches.

American Baptists had at last found a means of working together educationally. It was based on the total constituency, not just those moved to join a society; it was based on the needs of the student as well as the institution; and it was based on the needs of the local church and its membership. It was a new thing creatively devised. The tools of education for the training of the witnesses for Jesus Christ—both lay and professional—were now made available. Baptists could look forward with far greater confidence than their forefathers had been able to do a century before.

Eastern Baptist Theological Seminary

5. Disturbing the Witness

Theological
Controversy
and
Christian
Education

The second century of Baptist work in education and publication should have been entered with confidence, but theological tensions dictated otherwise. The fact that other mainstream religious bodies were doing no better than the American Baptists offered little comfort. That a worldwide economic depression seriously disrupted the business of the churches was really a side issue. The few denominations relatively unaffected by the modernist-fundamentalist struggle grew markedly; yet they faced the same economic pinch.

FUNDAMENTALIST INVESTIGATION

The crunch came first in the area of Christian higher education. As early as 1914, W. B. Riley, pastor of the large and influential First Baptist Church of Minneapolis, was raising serious questions about the wisdom of adopting the scientific approach to education in the Baptist colleges and seminaries. "So-called modern theology," he said, "is fish or fowl, as one prefers; an egg or a scorpion, as one has need" *(The Crisis of the Church,* p. 20). This cry of concern was joined by many others, and a call for action ensued. At the Convention in 1920 J. C. Massee, pastor of the Baptist Temple in

Brooklyn (which then had one of the largest congregations and church schools among Northern Baptists), offered a resolution to investigate the schools, colleges, and seminaries supported by Baptists. Prepared at the instigation of numerous fundamentalists over a period of years, the motion specified both the details of inquiry and the personnel of inquirers. The committee was to ascertain whether or not the schools and their faculties were loyal to principles Baptists had held in the past. Particularly mentioned were such doctrines as the inspiration of the Word of God, the deity of Christ, the atonement, the resurrection, the return of the Lord, the spiritual nature of the church, the necessity for a regenerated and baptized church membership, the unchanged nature of the obligation of the ordinances of baptism and the Lord's Supper, and the imperative of carrying out the Great Commission. Suggested membership for the committee of investigation included: F. M. Goodchild, New York; I. W. Carpenter, Omaha; J. W. Brougher, Los Angeles; Henry Bond, Brattleboro, Vermont; W. B. Riley, Minneapolis; C. R. Brock, Denver; E. S. Clinch, New York; A. K. deBlois, Boston; and J. J. Ross, Chicago. The character of the proposed committee was heavily pastoral and quite prominent.

The Convention listened to the resolution but was in no mood to hear what was being said. As Shailer Mathews was to write later, "The Modernist movement is a phase of the scientific struggle for freedom in thought and belief" *(The Faith of Modernism,* p. 22). It had little interest in historical theology and dogmatics, and even less patience. With fundamentalists in high indignation, it was clearly time for an ameliorating word to be heard. It was spoken by Dr. H. J. White of Hartford.

The substitute motion offered by Dr. White was a remarkable document. In it he stated: "Baptists have steadfastly contended for the competency of every soul in the sight of God, refusing to concur in the imposition of any doctrinal test by either political or ecclesiastical authority." The statement went on to reaffirm loyalty "to our Lord and Master," and to proclaim the gospel of Jesus Christ "in all its simplicity, purity, and power." The resolution urged the expression of "confidence in one another as brethren in Christ" and continued by declaring "we will not seek to have dominion over one another's faith . . . [and we will] seek to provoke one another to good works." Toward the conclusion the carefully worded statement called for the trustees and faculties of the various Baptist-supported schools to "examine their work, correct evils they may discover, and put forth a statement of their purpose and work which may give assurance to the denomination of their fidelity to the Saviour." Finally, he suggested that the persons named by Dr. Massee be appointed as the investigating committee.

The Massee resolution had aroused a storm of discussion and a clear division of the delegates. The substitute seemed at the moment to be a compromise worthy of Solomon. It passed with only one dissenting vote. Although Riley and Ross declined to serve, the committee roster was completed by the addition of pastors Sweet of Ohio and Twomey of New Jersey, and work was started at once.

The committee's method of approach took four broad avenues. First, they invited criticism from any and all. Second, a questionnaire consisting basically of five questions was addressed to the schools: (1) Was there any obligation by charter requiring trustees to be Baptist? (2) Likewise, faculty? (3) Was there any obligation that faculty believe and teach the inspiration of the Bible, the sinlessness of Jesus, the deity of Christ, the sufficiency of the atonement, the reality of the resurrection of Jesus Christ, the personality of the Holy Spirit, and the return of the Lord? (4) If there were any limiting legal obligations in accordance with the foregoing, were they being observed? (5) What were the religious activities currently a part of, the regular or extra curriculum?

In addition, a few of the committee personally visited some of the institutions, both collegiate and theological. By no means were all of the schools surveyed on campus. Finally, the seminaries were invited to present the record of achievement for their graduates in baptisms and contributions to missions. This data was compared with that assembled from the efforts of pastors not trained in Baptist schools. The results showed that Baptist-trained pastors had three times as many baptisms and their churches gave four times as much to missions as did the non-Baptist trained men. The voluminous report was signed by all members of the committee except Sweet. The document, which was called "a candid and judicial survey of conditions," was received unanimously by the Convention at Des Moines, an assembly noted in Baptist annals as not agreeing on much of anything. Yet this report seemed to meet a need. Mrs. Helen B. Montgomery, the Convention president, said: "That report will quiet many of your fears. . . . It found little to criticize and much to commend in all our schools . . . a clean bill of health."

The latter part of the president's statement was correct. The Committee did give the schools "a clean bill of health," but nothing could have been further from the truth than that it would quiet fears.

Several activities accompanied and followed the survey report. There was, first of all, a vigorous defense of the colleges and seminaries by the Board of Education, admitting that no institution was perfect, either. The Board stated that the theory of evolution and the principle of historical criticism of the Bible had broad acceptance and credibility and that to make these items points of issue was to move out of the field of religious faith. The fundamentalists did not agree.

They did see, however, that they had been outmaneuvered by the White resolution. It was never the intention for one Baptist to "have dominion" over another's faith. Although Baptists historically had objected to political authority over ecclesiastical structures, it was not true to suggest that Baptists had no theological fences. Their numerous confessions of faith spoke to that point. And in the use of those confessions, Baptists had employed them for guidance and for a banner around which to rally. It is true that Francis Wayland had depreciated the value of confessions of faith in his *Notes on the Principles and Practices of Baptist Churches,* but only on the basis that the plain statements of Scripture are sufficient, not on the basis of latitudinarianism. At the same time, Professor Sewell S. Cutting of Rochester was arguing for the validity of such confessions, and Jonathan Going and J. Newton Brown were framing the New Hampshire Confession, which became the foundation document for thousands of churches being established across the land (see chapter 2).

The fundamentalists quickly cried that the modernists were heretics because they refused to affirm and define their faith in historic terms. The modernists replied that the fundamentalists were hypocrites who wanted to substitute the Written Word for the living testimony. One commentator observed: "A good deal of the controversy between modernists and fundamentalists has been due to the want of a temperate, consistent, simple and clear statement of their respective positions" (U. M. McGuire, *The Baptist,* October 31, 1925).

It was Dr. Kenneth S. Latourette, then at Denison University and later at Yale, who defined the problem most adequately. He wrote: "Anyone who knows the history of American colleges cannot but view with alarm the tendency of institutions founded upon a Christian basis to become pagan in their tone. . . . The difficulty is not so much a change in the institutions' interpretation of the facts as of the increasing absence of the evidence of a genuinely Christian life." He spoke of the malady as "widespread and fatal." The solution of the problem demanded, he continued, a determination of the criteria by which to judge whether a college is becoming non-Christian, discovering the causes of deterioration, and finding and applying the remedy.

It can only be regretted that Dr. Latourette was not a member of the investigating committee. He was, at least, asking the right questions. However, under the strictures of the White resolution providing, in effect, for self-examination by the institutions themselves, perhaps nothing could have been accomplished. Be that as it may, three movements growing out of the unresolved controversy began to form. One was in theological education, one in evangelism, and one in church school curricula. All affected the Board of Education and the Publication Society.

THE NEW SEMINARIES

The first major reaction to surface was the establishment of new seminaries. The fundamentalists (who later preferred to be called "conservatives") concluded that if the older seminaries were not producing the type of ministerial graduate to suit them, they would establish schools that would do so. Dr. Harry W. Barras phrased the situation well when he said, "Between the schools that are liberal [a term coming into use as a substitute for modernist] in their teaching and the interdenominational schools that are turning into our ministry men who are Baptist in name, but not Baptist in loyalty, there is a wide, unoccupied space."

Eastern Baptist Theological Seminary. It was into this "unoccupied space" that a few men in New York and Pennsylvania decided to move. After a series of preliminary starts in 1924, a small group of six ministers met in the offices of the American Baptist Publication Society in Philadelphia and organized the Eastern Baptist Theological Seminary. Present at that meeting on March 19, 1925, were: Charles T. Ball, Wissinoming Church, Philadelphia; Harry W. Barras, the Publication Society; Groves W. Drew, Third Baptist, Philadelphia; Gordon H. Baker, First Church, Schenectady; John A. Hainer, Blockley Church, Philadelphia; and Ralph L. Mayberry,

Third Church, Germantown. These men, save Dr. Drew, agreed to serve as trustees of the projected school along with the following, previously committed or soon to be enlisted: John E. Briggs, Washington, D.C.; E. B. Dwyer, Kittanning, Pennsylvania; Frank Goodchild, Curtis Lee Laws, and Frank E. Parham, of New York; James A. Maxwell, Chester, Pennsylvania; David Lee Jamison, Albany, New York; P. Vanis Slawter, Trenton, New Jersey; and Thornley B. Wood, a Philadelphia businessman.

Three guidelines were to be strictly followed by the new seminary. It was to be cooperative with the Convention; it was to be in the mainstream of the historic Baptist theological position; and it was to be academically and scholastically sound. To accomplish these goals, a doctrinal basis was prepared and then affirmed by the trustees and faculty, a practice which has been observed annually ever since. The statement commends the Bible as "of supreme and final authority in faith and life." It supports the trinitarian position and acknowledges the virgin birth and the personality of the Holy Spirit. It accepts the fact of death through sin and life through the vicarious death of Christ. This was by no means as full a statement as the historic Baptist confessions of faith, but it was a step in clarification which many Baptists thought necessary. Others, of course, disagreed and therein lay the forces for conflict.

Equally exciting, and much more dramatic, was the result of a trip which Dr. Maxwell took in the spring of 1925 to California. He returned on May 28 to announce to a meeting of the trustees the gift of a half-million dollars. Although given anonymously, this fund was eventually attributed to the generosity of M. C. Treat, of Pasadena, who also gave generously to Linfield College, Redlands University, the Ministers and Missionaries Benefit Board, and the Home Mission Society. None of these institutions in any way directly perpetuates the Treat name, a policy continued by Mr. Treat's son-in-law, Dr. Gordon Palmer, who served a twelve-year period as president of Eastern Seminary.

With a full faculty and a substantial student body, Eastern Seminary was a thriving institution almost from the start. By 1970 the school had property valued at slightly less than two million dollars and an endowment in excess of three million. Enrollment was 180. During the period 1965–1970, four presidents of the American Baptist Convention were alumni of Eastern.

The collegiate division, still under the same president of the board

110

Eastern Baptist Theological Seminary, Philadelphia, Pennsylvania

American Baptist Seminary of the West

of trustees as the seminary, now functions most successfully as a largely independent unit under the name of Eastern College on a rolling shaded campus in St. Davids, Pennsylvania, on Philadelphia's suburban Main Line. In 1970 it had 508 students.

California Baptist Theological Seminary. The moderate theological position which had been taken by Berkeley Baptist Divinity School was not firm enough for some Baptists, however, and in 1944, under the leadership of Dr. Frederic I. Drexler, the California Baptist Theological Seminary was chartered and classes began in the Temple Baptist Church, Los Angeles, Dr. Kearney Keegan, pastor. Dr. Frank Kepner, executive secretary of the Southern California state convention, also lent his support. Others, more schismatic in temperament, attempted unsuccessfully to lead the school into the Conservative Baptist movement, then abandoned their interest in the project even though the school had a solidly fundamental statement of faith. Accreditation of the school, which had established its campus at Covina, was granted by the state convention in 1954 and by the American Baptist Convention four years later. Of special note is the fact that the first general secretary of the General Board of American Baptist Churches in the U.S.A. was Dr. Robert Campbell, who had been dean of the seminary at Covina for twenty-one years. This school in 1968 was merged with Berkeley Divinity School to form the American Baptist Seminary of the West (see chapter 4).

Northern Baptist Theological Seminary. Another of the stories of "new seminaries" originates at a much earlier date on the campus of the University of Chicago. This school was clearly designed to be the keystone in the Baptist educational arch in the Midwest. However, in less than twenty-five years its Divinity School became the center of tumultuous controversy as it kept in step with the rapidly changing pace in theology. In 1906, Professor George Foster of the Divinity School published his book *The Finality of the Christian Religion* espousing German rationalism, disclaiming the inspiration of the Bible, and questioning the deity of Christ. The Baptist Ministers' Conference, of which Foster was a member, ejected him, called upon him to resign from the ministry, and supported a resolution by Austen deBlois to the effect that the book was "contrary to the Scriptures and that its teachings and tendency are subversive of the vital and essential truths of the Christian faith." The vote on the resolution was forty-eight to twenty-two. The fact that six of the

twenty-two defenders were professors at the Divinity School told the story. They either agreed with Foster or accepted a sufficiently broad concept of academic freedom to support a latitudinarian policy toward theological education.

Two results of the revelation of the school's position followed rather promptly. Under the leadership of Dr. W. P. Throgmorton, of Marion, most of the churches of Southern Illinois left the state

114

convention, formed their own organization, and within one year numbered 386 churches (1907). Three years later they were firmly anchored in the Southern Baptist Convention. By 1970 this area numbered some 900 churches and contributed over two million dollars to missions.

The removal of the more outraged dissenters did not solve the problem. Baptists of the Midwest continued to be disturbed by the Divinity School, and in 1913 with the coming of Dr. John Marvin Dean to the pastorate of Second Baptist Church, matters were brought to a head. The Northern Baptist Theological Seminary was formed. Facilities were found in the Second Church edifice, a faculty appointed, and a student body gathered. The latter included some who were not college graduates but still felt the call to the ministry. The theological position of the school was set at the beginning in the mainstream of the historic Baptist thought. The New Hampshire Confession of Faith was received as standard, although in the early 1920s this was revised, strengthened, and shortened. Since 1927 the faculty and trustees have annually subscribed to the statement.

"Northern Baptist Theological Seminary," says James Mosteller, a former dean, "is graphically the shadow of two of its presidents." He was referring to Dr. George W. Taft and Dr. Charles Koller. The former served the school twenty years, and the latter twenty-four. Under their leadership, a splendid campus was built, a large student body attracted, and a full graduate-school status attained.

By 1969, however, it was clear that the neighborhood surrounding the school was so rapidly changing that the area was no longer satisfactory for a theological school. Furthermore, the pretheological department, still important for the training of students prior to their graduate divinity work, was proving to be a stumbling block in some academic circles. So with bold and sudden strokes, the trustees made several decisions. They would move the seminary. They would grant Dr. Koller early retirement (he hadn't had a sabbatical in twenty years), and they would ask Dr. Benjamin P. Browne of the Publication Society to become administrator.

The coming of Dr. Browne was accomplished by vigorous activity. The old campus was sold and a new location was secured at Oak Brook, Illinois. The college department was given independent status with a separate administration and board of trustees. A home for this new liberal arts college to be known as Judson, was found at Elgin, Illinois, and a new beautifully designed campus was built. In 1970,

Northern Seminary listed an enrollment of forty-five, occupied a lovely new campus valued at two million dollars, and had a current income of $367,000. In the same year Judson College had an enrollment of 360 students.

EVANGELISM

Another form of reaction which occurred as a direct result of the theological disturbance was a denomination-wide effort in evangelism. On May 27, 1926, on the occasion of the One-Hundred-Second Anniversary of the American Baptist Publication Society, Dr. J. C. Massee, then of Tremont Temple, Boston, addressed the Convention meeting of the Society on the subject "The Laodicean Lament." It was a moving experience. Dr. Massee had for years been a spokesman for the fundamentalists, but controversy was not his forte. He was, rather, a deeply courteous and profoundly sensitive southern gentleman. A gifted preacher, he had occupied some of the leading pulpits, both North and South. Disturbed by the incessant wrangling, he proposed to the Convention that attention be turned from theological debate to soul winning. For this he was termed a "turncoat" by Dr. Riley and some of the more militant fundamentalists, but Massee bore the attack with Christian grace. While the fundamentalists split only to group and regroup later, the call to witnessing fell on listening ears.

Following Dr. Massee's address, Dr. J. W. Brougher, of Temple Church, Los Angeles, moved that the suggestion for evangelism be pursued. His motion was adopted with general approbation, and a committee of fifteen was appointed to implement the idea. Two and possibly three streams of effort were released by this decision.

First, the Publication Society in 1927 offered prizes of $500, $300, and $200 for the three best book manuscripts presented to them for publication on the general theme of evangelism. Under this stimulus there appeared such volumes as: *The Real Jesus,* by James A. Francis; *Soul Trapping and Other Sermons,* by John Snape; and *The Evangelistic Church,* by Frederick E. Taylor. This program was continued for four years and then halted. The reason or reasons for such cessation do not appear in the records beyond the cryptic word "misunderstanding." Perhaps sensitive and talented preachers couldn't stand coming in second, or third! Nevertheless, the Publication Society did maintain a vigorous policy of publishing evangelistic material of varying types.

More spectacular were the evangelistic conferences sponsored by the Society and led by Dr. Massee and by Dr. Samuel Neil, secretary of the Bible and Field Department. A series of meetings was held in Minnesota, Nebraska, Colorado, Iowa, and Ohio. Here in the heartland of America the response in both attendance and interest was gratifying. So splendid, indeed, was the reaction that Dr. Massee was later led to resign his pulpit to devote the major portion of his time to the task of itinerant evangelism.

Meanwhile, Dr. Neil was also keeping his eye on the colporter and chapel-car work. He joyously reported concerning the efforts of Rev. and Mrs. John L. Losh: "In one family the father was restored from a backslidden condition and four of his children, two girls and two boys ranging in age from twelve to twenty-four, believed and were saved." In another context, Dr. Neil asked, "If unconverted people will not come to us, should we not go to them?"

In other areas of the Society's responsibility, emphasis was placed likewise on evangelism. The Religious Education Department was convinced "that the evangelism of youth is a first obligation upon the church" and called upon teachers and workers to train for this essential task. The Department of Sunday School Publications was concerned also and noted that all their writers were required to "be true to the Word of God."

One might conclude that the fundamentalists should have been pacified with these honest efforts in the area so dear to their hearts—the winning of the lost. Clearly, evangelism was a major concern to them, and they practiced what they preached, but it was not their only concern. They were also interested in theology, and no amount of evangelism could cover the fact that some Baptist leaders clearly did not hold to the faith of their fathers. So in 1933 the fundamentalists again raised their heads, and this time they were bringing into review the doctrinal character of the Sunday school literature. For the next decade, this was an item frequently found on the agenda. How could both liberals and conservatives be served by one publishing house and one educational agency? The answer to this question was long in coming and tortuously arrived at.

THE LITERATURE CONTROVERSY

The problems which the fundamentalists were raising were anything but new. Twenty-eight years before, the issues had appeared in the University of Chicago Divinity School disturbance with the

117

resulting schism of the southern Illinois churches. Thirteen years before, the spectre of theological dispute had arisen in the investigative study of the denomination's colleges and seminaries. With the establishment of a group of new schools cast in the more doctrinally orthodox mold, it should have been recognized that the problem was set, but the Publication Society didn't see the situation thus. True, merchandise and periodical sales were down from $776,854 in 1925 to $438,894 in 1934. This drop was due, it was explained, to economic reasons. The Depression, of course, was a contributing factor, but the disaffection of hundreds of churches, including the development of the General Association of Regular Baptists and other schismatic groups, should have been honestly recognized. It was not. Instead, the offical report for 1934 stated: "In asking the churches to use the materials prepared by the Society, the appeal is not based solely upon what we conceive to be denominational loyalty; it is based also upon our conviction that Baptist schools prosper most and serve best when they use Baptist literature, and the publications of the Society, item by item, are the equal of and in most cases superior to those published by other denominations or by non-denominational. independent publishing houses." Such myopia was to prove costly.

One thing had changed, and that was the ability of the fundamentalists to obtain a hearing. The Board minutes for 1934 are replete with references to the situation. The opening approach was made by the concerned. The fundamentalists had requested copies of the entire Sunday school curriculum series for one year. This they proposed to study and analyze for evidences of orthodoxy, or otherwise, and report with "chapter and verse" to the Society. The advantage of such an approach would be obvious. All could see what was being questioned and evaluate the degree of bias in the changes.

Unfortunately, the matter was not that simple. In the first place, the amount of literature to be screened was too great. One quarter's supply would have to suffice. Furthermore, the professional competence of the examiners must be noted. They were not trained educators and editors; they were pastors with large and active churches. The time factor alone to review the material would be burdensome. Nevertheless, a committee of twenty-two was organized; responsibilities were divided and assigned; and the work was started.

Early in 1934 the report of the fundamentalists was ready to be presented to the Board. Three of the committee came as a delegation: Dr. John W. Bradbury, a New York pastor soon to be associated with Curtis Lee Laws and *The Watchman-Examiner;* Dr. Carey Thomas, of Altoona, Pennsylvania; and Dr. J. Whitcomb Brougher, former president of the Convention. Bradbury, as spokesman for the group, presented the very extensive report. This report with its numerous references to specific items and ideas in the literature was received with thanks by the Board and referred to the Sunday School Publications Committee for review and judgment. The fundamentalists were as polite as the Board; each thanked the other! It appeared that the days of the Des Moines and Seattle Conventions were long past, that a time of peace and judicious calm was pervading the denomination, that the critics were being reasonable, and the officials were being sensitive. Nothing could have been further from the truth!

The inability of the Board members to hear what was being said to them may be indicated by the next item on their agenda. They went into executive session and arranged the cutback of the Boston store. The employees there were reduced from thirteen to six, and those remaining were to be given a short course in the promotion of curriculum materials. "They will familiarize themselves with the good points of our Keystone Graded Courses, our Uniform Lesson helps, and all of our periodicals in order that they may not only answer criticisms but also help workers to see how they may use these materials to the best advantage."

A preliminary answer to the fundamentalists was prepared by Editor Miles W. Smith for the Board at the March meeting. It was stated that "some of the charges made . . . were not supported by the exhibit." However, every suggestion was considered and the editors would try to implement the helpful recommendations. This statement was accepted by the Board and the editorial committee was instructed to complete its work.

At the May meeting of the Board, the fundamentalists were answered more fully. Their efforts were appreciated, it was declared, as constructive criticisms were always welcomed. Criticisms were nothing new, of course; they recalled how it was a generation ago when people didn't want the Uniform Lessons. The editors were also surprised at the condemnatory tone so often taken by the critics. This must be due, they argued, to a misunderstanding of the purpose of "our periodicals" and an honest difference of opinion as to what constitutes good educational method. Seeming theological differences represented merely a confusion of terminology, not an essential disagreement. Furthermore, there was a lot of good doctrine taught in the material not examined. Finally, the editors believed that little profit could come through debate over controversial matters and that a little charity on both sides would help.

In this reaction the Society almost wholly ignored the issues. Here were thousands of customers trying to tell the reasons for their unhappiness with a product, but the producers were missing the point. Self-righteousness, side issues, and educational methodology would not deal with the theological concerns that had been troubling fundamentalists for a generation.

The fundamentalists had charged in their report that while some of the Sunday school materials retained a "conservative and evangelical basis, yet there is mixed in with this material a considerable amount of troublesome and adventurous interpretations of Scripture which far from clarifying the truth, rather lead to complex and inharmonious conclusions." They continued by charging that there was "little in this literature [that] could cause either a Jew or a Unitarian to see the need of being saved." The concluding suggestion was that the Publication Society should not mix liberal and conservative theological ideas in one set of curriculum materials.

Since the Society was functioning from a unified stance, and since the churches were most diverse—in culture, in theology, in educational sophistication, in social outlook, in evangelistic concerns and presuppositions—it was apparent that no meeting of the minds would be achieved. Editor Smith gave a long personal testimony concerning his own firm convictions in the faith. No one doubted these. He was much loved and respected, but the apologetic missed the mark. He was not on trial; the literature was. Nevertheless, the Board sustained him and turned aside from the fundamentalists. It would continue to publish literature under one philosophy and one theology intended to be broad enough to cover all types and kinds of churches. Talented pastors could, of course, take measures which would allow satisfactory use of the materials in churches which did not fit the pattern—measures such as special training for their teachers and the addition of extra source material—but many were equipped neither professionally nor attitudinally for this. The result was a further decline of $95,043 in sales of merchandise and periodicals.

Some new directions were taken. In 1936, after years of negotiation, the three youth efforts—the B.Y.P.U., the Youth Department of the Board of Education, and the Youth Division of the Publication Society—were brought together in a unified program. In 1937, some Sunday school material was published as a joint effort with the Disciples of Christ, a cooperative procedure that was to become more and more common.

By 1938, however, the situation had deteriorated to the point of serious concern. The Committee on Sunday School Publications was moved to make another examination of its products. This time the work was done by Henry E. Cole, a neutral professional, rather than as a self study. His report was devastating. It was declared that the greatest weakness in the Publication Society had been the failure to serve the people through the Sunday school literature. The investigator noted that the churches demanded a greater biblical and evangelistic emphasis than was being provided. He went into a thoroughly professional analysis of each periodical to prove his point, much as the fundamentalists had done five years previously.

Needless to say, the Cole report was shocking to many in the Society, and a field test of 173 churches was thereupon taken in the states of Oregon and Washington. This showed that 30 percent were not buying ABPS material at all; 50 percent were fair customers; and 20 percent were rated excellent. The field report went on to observe that (1) teacher training, so stressed by the denomination, had not made a dent in improving or securing teachers; (2) much more material was needed for beginning teachers in their texts; (3) there was a general feeling that boys and girls in Baptist Sunday schools were getting a "scant knowledge of the Bible"; and (4) there was need for more personal contact between the society and the smaller churches. In other words, the Society was serving fewer and fewer churches in a better and better fashion.

This was an intolerable situation for an organization with a mission of mass merchandising. The fundamentalists had been saying this for years and had been withdrawing either within themselves or from the denomination as a whole. The resulting fragmentations did nobody any good. Some drastic action was called for. The witness, so clearly enunciated a century and more before, had now become a confused and disordered testimony. What was to be done?

6. Arousing *the Witnes*

A Period of Renewed Unity and Enthusiasm

It was a beautiful day in the summer, 1938, at Rittenhouse Square, Philadelphia, and the class in Philosophy of Religion at Eastern Baptist Seminary had assembled at the regular hour in their classroom adjoining the square, but the professor was late. Just as the normal instincts of youth were about to take control and dismiss the class for more timely pursuits, he hurried in. Dr. David Lee Jamison, who had been a lawyer before he became a minister, was normally the epitome of sagacious calmness and polite promptness. But this time he was excited and a bit flustered. He had a story and could hardly wait to share it. He had just come from a meeting of the Board of Managers of the Publication Society at their headquarters a few blocks away at 1701 Chestnut Street. They had voted to call a new executive secretary for the Society and he had accepted. Luther Wesley Smith was on his way! It was Dr. Jamison's enthusiastic conviction that a Moses had been found to lead the American Baptists out of their wilderness wanderings into the Promised Land. He was to be proved right.

THE MAN AND HIS MINISTRY

Luther Wesley Smith had a way with people. Thoroughly

123

gregarious but not aggressively offensive, remarkably brilliant but not stuffily academic, an activist but with a strongly pragmatic direction, the new executive secretary of the Society was to become a mover of mountains and a maker of plains that Baptists had not seen in a long, long time. He was well prepared for his role. He was the son of a Massachusetts Baptist pastor, Rev. Wesley L. Smith. His education was obtained at the Latin School, Harvard University *(cum laude),* and Andover Newton Theological School. Add to this a tour of duty as a Navy ensign during World War I, and his background represented (for New Englanders, at least) the best of all possible educational worlds.

Following seminary, his evident talent carried him to the distinguished pulpit of the First Baptist Church of Columbia, Missouri. Handsome, magnetic, and unmarried, the young preacher must have caused many a heartthrob among the young ladies of nearby Stephens College. With the Columbia church dually aligned with both Northern and Southern Conventions, another dimension was added to Smith's ministry. The warm-hearted evangelism of the southerners and the impressive programs of their summer assemblies at Ridgecrest, North Carolina, at which the Columbia pastor was a frequent speaker, made deep and lasting impressions. These were later to surface in such movements as the Church School Advance and the American Baptist Assembly at Green Lake, Wisconsin (see chapter 7).

Meanwhile, the pastor was sharpening his skills as a fund raiser by leading in the erection of a splendid student center at Columbia for the youth of Stephens College and the University of Missouri. In the process of this campaign, he visited every county in the state and personally interviewed hundreds of potential donors.

Such marked activity and achievement could not go unnoticed by other churches, especially those with vacant pulpits. So it was that in 1934, at the age of nearly thirty-seven years, Luther Wesley Smith moved to the pastorate of the First Baptist Church, Syracuse, New York, a large downtown institution with a scattered congregation whose edifice included a hotel. Erected under the "business plus church plan," the structure was designed, as were some others of the period, to enable the church to stay in the heart of the city and to gain financial support from the use of its property. Unfortunately, this plan did not always prove workable. Instead of the office or hotel building carrying the church, the reverse was likely to be true.

Certainly such was the case in Syracuse. The church found itself with a $300,000 debt, and the nation was in the grip of depression. The situation was made to order for the new pastor. The congregation was revitalized; the mortgage was brought under control; and the church budget began to show a balance. As an organizer, promoter, fund raiser, and herald of enthusiasm for Christ's enterprises, Luther Wesley Smith knew few peers. It was to this man that the Publication Society turned in 1938—in its time of trial—and it was not disappointed.

ENLIVENING THE SUNDAY SCHOOL

In 1926, shortly after celebrating its Centennial, the Society had been so confident of its economic security that it had voluntarily withdrawn from participation in the denominational missionary budget. At that time it was self-supporting and proud of it. Sadly, however, by the late thirties, losses were approximately $60,000 per year. As the new executive reviewed the situation, he concluded that only one more year was left to the Society to put its house in order. He called for action.

Four steps must be taken promptly, he said. These were: (1) retrench in both program and staff; (2) adjust policies to conform to economic facts and trends; (3) seek and secure a larger measure of loyalty from those churches through which the buying power of Northern Baptists was being dissipated; and (4) become reinstated in the Unified Budget to the extent of closing the gap between balanced and deficit financing. To keep an extra tight rein on affairs, Smith had himself appointed acting business manager of the Society, and for professional expertise he brought to his side a young Philadelphia businessman, George Moll. Mr. Moll, an active churchman, was the founder and president of George Moll Advertising, Inc. He had been a member of Alpha Baptist Church in the city since his youth and had been well trained by a great pastor, Howard K. Williams. Mr. Moll was an expert in the areas of promotion and business management.

Another key lieutenant whose abilities were captured was Richard Hoiland, a native of Bergen, Norway, who had come with his mother to the United States at the age of eight years. He had been educated at Bethel Academy, Macalester College, and at the University of Chicago. At the Divinity School of the University he had specialized in religious education. After a time as director of young people's work for the Baptists of Minnesota, he was, in 1930,

ACHIEVEMENT CHART
FOR BAPTIST SUNDAY SCHOOLS

1 A *Church* SCHOOL
The Sunday school shall be related organically to the church through a committee or board created by the church which shall be responsible for planning and directing the total teaching program of the church. This board shall make regular reports to the church.

2 A *Bible* SCHOOL
The Bible shall be basic in all the teaching of the school, and Bibles shall be used in every department and class.

3 A *Baptist* SCHOOL
The distinctive principles and the worldwide ministry of American Baptists shall be taught through the use of American Baptist teaching materials in every department.

4 AN *Evangelistic* SCHOOL
The spirit of evangelism shall motivate the teaching of the school. The school shall (1) carry through a definite plan for winning each pupil to Christ; and (2) co-operate with the pastor in providing special training for discipleship and church membership.

5 A *Missionary* SCHOOL
The school shall co-operate with the missionary, educational and benevolent program of American Baptists; and at least four denominational causes shall be presented to the school annually.

6 A *Growing* SCHOOL
The school shall increase the number of those in attendance by at least 5 per cent for the year.

7 A *Graded* SCHOOL
The school shall be graded according to the age groups described below and pupils shall be taught in one or more separate classes for each age group, to the extent that physical equipment and enrollment permit. The school shall maintain a Standard Home Department. The American Baptist standard for grading the Sunday church school is: Nursery (including home cribs), birth through 3; Kindergarten, 4-5; Primary, 6-8; Junior, 9-11; Junior High (Intermediates), 12-14; Senior, 15-17; Young People, 18-24; Young Adult, 25-35; Adult, 36 and up.

8 A *Planned* SCHOOL
The school shall plan its total program through at least nine workers' conferences held during the year, and attended by not less than 60 per cent of the teachers and officers.

9 A *Leader-trained* SCHOOL
The school shall hold or participate in at least one standard leadership training class or school and at least 25 per cent of the school's teachers and officers shall have earned, through any recognized method, one or more standard leadership training credits during the year.

10 A *Church-going* SCHOOL
At least 75 per cent of those in attendance upon the church school and above the Primary Department shall attend the morning worship service of the church.

Refer to the "GUIDE to the Use of the Achievement Chart" for explanation of the ten points. As each point is achieved, mount one of the gummed "√" stickers in the square alongside the point on the chart.

To become an "A" School of the American Baptist Convention, achieve all ten points on the chart within one convention year; fill out the Information Return contained in the "GUIDE" and mail it to the Division of Education in Home, Church and Community, 1703 Chestnut Street, Philadelphia 3, Pa. After proper accrediting of the return, you will be notified concerning the award of the "A" Banner to your school.

The Successful Church School Reaches, Teaches, Wins, Enlists and Trains

made director of young people's work for the Society. He was a talented student of the whole field of Christian education and a sensitive observer of the local church situation. That he was also a first-rate raconteur of humorous tales may be a bit beside the point here, but the gift often came in handy during his years with the Society. Later, from 1952 to 1956, he was to serve as associate executive secretary of the Society; and from 1956 to 1964 as executive secretary. He was also to be the guiding spirit in the moving of American Baptist national offices to Valley Forge, Pennsylvania, in 1962.

This remarkable trio came, in the providence of God, to give the educational work of American Baptists a mighty revival. They came

126

not as prima donna individualists, but as a closely integrated team which would give dynamic and effective leadership.

The first tangible evidence of the new thrust in Christian education was the Baptist Church School Advance, introduced in 1940 as World War II was spreading across Europe. This was a two-year denomination-wide Sunday school increase campaign. Overall, the program had as its goals: to increase Baptist church school attendance by 10 percent in each of two succeeding years, to reinstitute the importance of Christian education in the ministry of the local church, and to give something "that will appeal to all groups within our denomination and which will exert a very direct and wholesome influence on the spiritual life of our churches everywhere."

To achieve these ambitious and worthy aims, five challenges were put before the local churches. "Reach all you can for Christ," "Teach all you reach," "Win all you teach," "Enlist all you win," and "Train all you enlist." In bright, bold posters church members from Maine to California were made aware of a stirring. Here were brave, clear notes of a trumpet call to action. The days of the genteel nudge, the pious pleading, the worrisome hand wringing were over. American Baptists were being summoned by no uncertain sound.

A sixteen-page booklet, *Somber Shadows,* was assembled to tell the story of "what is wrong with the world—what is the cure." With attention-grabbing graphic art the "Shadows over America," the "Shadows over Home," and the "Shadows over Youth" were illustrated. The world had become a dismal place. Life was often drab and frequently frustrating, but these things really did not need to be. The causes were known. They were selfishness—"the Shadow in the Heart"—and the loss of spiritual power in the church—"Is there a Shadow over the Church?" Obviously there was, and it was the responsibility of the church to remind the world, and itself, that "most of the institutions and movements that aim to elevate mankind" had their origin in the Christian enterprise. In the passage of time, Christ the source of motivating reformation power had been forgotten. The cure, then was for the church to reassert its rightful place as the releasing agent of God's power in Christ. With banners flowing and colors streaming, this was precisely what the Publication Society challenged its constituency to do.

Seldom, if ever, had the denomination seen such a frontal, professionally designed, and pertinent attack upon its problems. The matters that united Baptists would be emphasized rather than those which divided. The appeal would be Christ-centered and highly motivated. It would be an evangelistic Christian education crusade.

The strategy was blessed with success. More than 3,800 churches enrolled in the program by 1942, accounting for more than 80 percent of American Baptists. Measured in business terms, the Society reported net operating income of $13,333 compared with a net loss for 1937 of $62,192. Baptists were being given a lively, workable program, and they were responding to the crusade with commendable enthusiasm.

One goal, crucially important, was not being achieved, however. In his 1944 report to the Convention, Richard Hoiland with commendable candor remarked that his records showed a net loss in Baptist Sunday school enrollment of 132,913 between the years 1940 and 1943, the time of the Church School Advance. This sorry report, however, merely challenged the staff to new creativity. The Church School Enlargement Campaign was brought forth from the Advance and launched among the churches.

In the new program the best features of the earlier thrust were to be maintained, plus an extra effort upon outreach. In March, 1943, twenty churches in Philadelphia cooperated in a field test program with enough positive results to encourage broader effort. In September an enlargement campaign was sponsored in Rochester with twenty-five churches participating. In the space of one Sunday afternoon, 1,100 callers went out on a religious census and reported the findings of 6,000 prospects for the churches. During the same season, similar crusades were launched in Portland (Oregon), Seattle, and Wichita. All reported much enthusiasm, many prospects for the church school, and much good gained. To direct this program called for more hands than were available at headquarters. A director was found in Rev. Frank E. Johnston, who was called out of a pastorate at the First Baptist Church, Middletown, Ohio, after considerable success in his own church with the Church School Advance. Johnston was to head the newly created Division of Church School Administration. Later his diligence was to lead to service as General Secretary of the entire denomination.

The instrument which Johnston introduced as the central feature of Church School Enlargement became known as the Achievement Plan. It featured ten goals which churches were challenged to attain, and those who accomplished all ten were awarded a pennant bearing a large letter "A" (inspired, perhaps, by the "E" for excellence pennants the U. S. Government had been awarding for outstanding service by contractors in the war effort).

The goals were anything but easy to reach. They were:

1. A CHURCH SCHOOL
   The Sunday school shall be related organically to the church through a committee or board created by the church which shall be responsible for planning and directing the total teaching program of the church. This board shall make regular reports to the church.
2. A BIBLE SCHOOL
   The Bible shall be basic in all the teaching of the school, and Bibles shall be used in every department and class.
3. A BAPTIST SCHOOL
   The distinctive principles and the worldwide ministry of Northern Baptists shall be taught through the use of Northern Baptist teaching materials in every department.
4. AN EVANGELISTIC SCHOOL
   The spirit of evangelism shall motivate the teaching of the school. The school shall (1) carry through a definite plan for winning each pupil to Christ; and (2) cooperate with the pastor in providing special training for discipleship and church membership.
5. A MISSIONARY SCHOOL
   The school shall cooperate with the missionary, educational, and benevolent program of Northern Baptists; and at least four denominational causes shall be presented to the school annually.
6. A GROWING SCHOOL
   The school shall increase the number of those in attendance by at least 5 percent for the year.
7. A GRADED SCHOOL
   The school shall be graded according to the age group described below and the pupils shall be taught in one or more separate classes for each age group to the extent that physical equipment and enrollment permit. The Northern Baptist standard for grading the Sunday church school is: Nursery (including Cradle Roll), birth through 3; Beginners, 4-5; Primary, 6-8; Junior, 9-11; Junior High (Intermediate), 12-14; Senior, 15-17; Young People, 18-24; Young Adults, 25-36 (approximately); Adults, 37 and up.
8. A PLANNED SCHOOL
   The school shall plan its total program through at least nine workers' conferences held during the year, and attended by not less than 60 percent of the teachers and officers.
9. A LEADER-TRAINED SCHOOL
   The school shall hold or participate in at least one standard leadership training class or school and at least 25 percent of the school's teachers and officers shall have earned, through any recognized method, one or more standard leadership training credits during the year.
10. A CHURCH-GOING SCHOOL
    At least 75 percent of those in attendance in the church school and in age groups above the Primary Department shall attend the morning worship service of the church.

"The Achievement Plan," wrote Frank Johnston in an early report, "is not a temporary promotion scheme, but rather a long-range plan." He admitted that some church schools would "need several years to have their first experience of achieving all ten goals in one year." The new director was right. In 1948, a total of thirty-seven Sunday church schools earned the "A" pennant and the Emblem of Achievement by attaining all the goals. For twelve of the churches this was a new experience. For five it had been an annual accomplishment since the plan's introduction five years earlier: Norwood church, Norwood, Ohio; First church, Lancaster, Pennsylvania; North Springfield church, North Springield, Vermont; Lumberport church, Lumberport, West Virginia; and First church, Lovell, Wyoming.

Pastors and Christian educators recognized the value of the aims and aspirations for the local church school so brilliantly and succinctly outlined here. The fact that the vast majority of Baptist schools won no star of recognition contributed no sense of frustration or defeat. Most people understood the plan for its daring challenges; most of the churches made some attempt at achievement; and most were helped by it.

Another church educational outreach in evangelism was the program known as Winning the Children for Christ, an outgrowth of a Christian education conference held in Franklin, Indiana, on December 28–31, 1941. Present were sixty-eight delegates from twenty-two states along with other representatives from various bodies of the denomination. The discussion highlighted ten steps through which a child is led into a full relationship to God through Jesus Christ. The developed plan called for evangelism in the home and an accompanying program in the church, but it focused on neighborhood gatherings for children. Field workers would be engaged for local area instruction and demonstration schools. Hundreds of lay workers would be trained. Attractive and appropriate literature would be prepared. Miss Lois Blankenship, director of Christian education at the very large First Baptist Church, Wichita, was brought in to administer the program. Funding came from the Home Mission Societies as well as the Publication Society. In time, thousands of children would be helped and brought to Christ.

It would have seemed that the vigorous approach to church problems that Luther Wesley Smith brought to the Publication Society would have stifled the cries of the critics. He was a diligent peacemaker and a dynamic and creative administrator. There was certainly nothing in the various church school advancement campaigns about which the conservatives (as the fundamentalists had then come to be known) could complain. These campaigns were Christ-centered; they were evangelistic; they were local church oriented; they were practical; and they rode a crest of enthusiasm not often presented in religious programs. Unfortunately, this was not enough. The fissure in American Baptist fellowship which appeared in the very early 1940s did not vanish. It continued to enlarge and by the close of the decade was an established fact. The Conservative Baptist Association and its various allied affiliations in home and foreign missions soon numbered thousands of supporters in over twelve hundred churches. Probably not a state convention was left untouched. It was a battle that not even Luther Wesley Smith and a rejuvenated Publication Society could win.

THE UNION WITH THE BOARD OF EDUCATION

It was no help to the conservative wing of the Convention that a union was finally achieved between the Publication Society and the Board of Education. It was, however, the resolution of numerous difficulties in the denomination at large. Both the Board and the Society were engaged in educational activities, and both ministered to the same constituency of churches. Both were under the aegis of one denomination. Both were concerned with the Christian education of youth, and both felt a responsibility for education in mission. Clearly something more than bureaucratic cooperation was called for. The exigencies of a situation brought matters to a head.

In 1940, after leading the Board of Education since 1912, Dr. Padelford reached retirement age. With no replacement in sight, the next year Dr. Smith was asked to assume executive responsibility for the Board. This, of course, was in addition to his already onerous duties at the Publication Society. In his judgment and that of many others, it was best to bring the two organizations together. His aim was the development of "one coordinated program of Christian and missionary education for the churches through one national staff." Whether it was education in church school, college, divinity school, or youth society, it was education—Christian education—and could and should be administered by one board of directors and one staff.

Setting earnestly to work, Dr. Smith soon had the two staffs working as departments under one administration, and in 1942 he brought together the two Boards of Managers for a comprehensive work session. By May, 1944, the two agencies, which had begun so differently and progressed so variously, had discovered a commonality which augured well for a congenial future. So the Convention approved the merger and the Board of Education and Publication become a reality. Seldom had Baptists been able to achieve such unity so promptly; the marriage seemed to be a natural. Much of the credit must go to Dr. Smith, who was willing to experiment and test a proposal before insisting on its adoption.

The merged Board had its share of problems. American Baptist educational institutions were wholly independent organizations. Nevertheless, they were Baptist in origin and Baptist in tradition and looked to the Baptist constituency for support. The colleges laid a broad foundation of liberal arts with a Christian basis, and the seminaries prepared the Baptist clergy professionally. Clearly both were integral to the Baptist enterprise, but the connection between the institutions and the constituency was mainly financial, and this was practiced largely on an individual basis. Since dollars bear no denominational imprimatur—Presbyterian money pays as many salaries and buys as many buildings as Baptist money—and since the schools were always in need, sometimes desperately, they took the logical course of soliciting and accepting funds from all donors. Thus, Baptists found themselves in the process of losing what little control they ever had of their schools.

The Board of Education had, of course, been dealing with the problem for years. Under Dr. Smith these efforts were intensified. He felt, and rightly so, that "the cause of Christian higher education must be brought more intimately into the life of the churches" and, further, that the denomination should begin the direct channeling of funds to the institutions. In other words, it was Smith's concept that the colleges and seminaries in the United States were as legitimately a part of the missionary program of the Baptist people as those on the foreign field. The first tangible result of this policy was the inclusion by the Convention finance committee of an item for the schools in a special campaign drive called the World Emergency Forward Fund. With the social catastrophe of World War II and the evident needs arising therefrom, the new leader of the Board of Education was correctly emphasizing comparable needs in higher education. Of the total sum raised, nearly $200,000 was for education. Divided among the recipients, this was a modest amount indeed, but it was significant.

Early in his administration, Smith turned to professionals for advice in fund raising. As a result, a long relationship with the firm of Marts and Lundy was established. Mr. Marts, the son of a Congregational minister and a member of Norman Vincent Peale's Marble Collegiate Church, New York, had a long and successful career in philanthropic financing. He was then (1941) president of Bucknell University and was, or had been, a trustee of Wilkes College, Woods Hole Oceanographic Institution, Oberlin College, and Bradford Junior College. Clearly he had wide experience in higher education, and his achievements in fund raising were phenomenal. One of his first partners in the firm of Marts and Lundy was a Philadelphia lawyer by the name of Louis W. Robey, a Baptist to whom fell much of the direct responsibility of guiding his denomination during the next generation in an intense search for capital funds. In fact, Dr. Smith established a new department in the organization of the Board of Education and hired Robey as director. Not long after, Paul C. Carter was added as assistant, and the trio—Smith, Robey, and Carter—went to work on the needs of Christian higher education much as the team of Smith, Hoiland, and Moll attacked the Sunday school problem.

In May, 1943, there was launched the New Development Program under the chairmanship of James L. Kraft and three hundred other prominent American Baptists. Mr. Kraft was a self-made Chicago businessman who had risen from a cheese salesman with one horse and wagon to the presidency of his own industrial empire. He was superintendent of the Sunday school at the North Shore Baptist Church, Chicago, and a longtime trustee of Northern Baptist Seminary. He knew at firsthand the needs and the worth of Christian higher education. The selection of Mr. Kraft as lay leader of the campaign was a wise one. Approximately five million dollars was raised over a five-year period. Never before had American Baptists gathered such a sum for such a purpose from so many supporters.

The year following, 1944, saw the establishment of the National Scholarship and Loan Fund. Early in the New Development Program it was found that only one in six Baptists had gone to college. One reason was lack of student-aid funds. One result was a lack of trained leadership in church and community. The solution to the problem of lifting Baptists from a position of mediocrity was obvious—help more youth to receive an education. On the broad basis of denominational support hundreds of Baptist youth would be assisted financially in obtaining a college-level education. This, in turn, would also help the Baptist colleges by sending them students with money in hand. It was an astute plan which served for a quarter of a century to benefit some three thousand American Baptist youth who were aided by scholarship grants from the invested funds of about $1,600,000.

Schools and colleges related to the Board at this period in history were a large and varied group. There were 8 seminaries for the general professional training of ministers, with an enrollment of 1,457 and total endowment of $13,070,395. In addition, there were 4 seminaries ministering to specific ethnic groups (Swedish, German, Norwegian, and Spanish) with a combined enrollment of 322 and property valued at $373,727. There were 2 women's training schools for Christian workers, having a student enrollment of about 100 and an endowment of $267,000. There were 19 colleges in the North with a total student body of 13,259 and a supporting endowment of just under a hundred million dollars. Junior colleges to the number of 10 were listed. Here, over 4,000 students were enrolled and an income of $3,520,680 undergirded the endeavor. There were 9 academies or prep schools with an enrollment of over 1,500 and an income of a million dollars a year. Colleges in the South especially designed for the Black constituency numbered 10. There were 3,614 students enrolled and the institutions reported an income of $1,233,285. From these last 10 schools have come the great majority of the Black leadership in our American Baptist family today and in the social reformation of our times.

All in all, nearly 25,000 students were enrolled. Supporting endowment amounted to about 125 million dollars. This was a tremendous educational thrust. To what extent would Baptists be able to support it? Luther Wesley Smith and his aides would do their best. Would it be enough?

Before major attention could be devoted to educational fund raising, however, there was another priority. The devastation of World War II and the accumulated unfulfilled needs of the depression years had created a tremendous backlog of buildings to be repaired or rebuilt and programs to be initiated, reorganized, or restarted, on the home front and throughout the world wherever American Baptist work existed. As a result American Baptists determined upon a great fund-raising campaign known as the World Mission Crusade and called upon Luther Wesley Smith to lead it.

At that time Dr. Smith was, in effect, executive officer of the Board of Education, executive officer of the Publication Society, manager of the business department of the Society, member of the Convention's Council on Finance and Promotion, a member of the CFP's administrative committee, and a prime mover in the Green Lake Assembly. Such a full portfolio demanded full cooperation from his coworkers. This he received. To Newton C. Fetter, who had been associated with the Board of Education through its campus-ministry program for many years, fell the task of administering the work of the New York office, that is, education. To Richard Hoiland, secretary of the Christian education department, there was given the direction of the work of the Philadelphia office, that is, the Publication Society. With "only occasional visits to the Board's offices in New York or Philadelphia," wrote Dr. Smith in his report to the Convention, he had been able to keep in touch with the work of the Board and to confer with his aides on major policy. To their credit as managers, and his as overseer, the work proceeded well.

Meanwhile, Luther Smith was busy going about the country bringing into being a large and vigorous organization geared to the raising of a fund of $14,000,000. Prominent laymen had to be found and committed to the proposition. They must lend their names, give their time, and donate their money. Leading pastors must be convinced of the project and provided with support and guidance. A corps of talented field men must be gathered, trained, and directed in the actual operation. Louis W. Robey, of course, with his specialists from Marts and Lundy, would provide the technical assistance. C. Oscar Johnson, the great-hearted pastor from Third Church, St. Louis, would be there with his counsel and supporting influence. Governor Harold Stassen would be there. So would George Moll and James L. Kraft. Luther Smith would have lots of help, and he would need it all.

Baptists heard the word; they got the message; and they responded magnificently. The World Mission Crusade became "the most successful fund-raising effort in the history" of American Baptists. The goal was more than reached. The total amount came to more than $16,000,000. Luther Wesley Smith found some secrets of unity and strength that the denomination had long been searching for. Thus he brought new vigor to all the agencies of the Convention, including his own, the Board of Education and Publication.

Judson Tower
at Green Lake

7. Inspiring the Witnes.

Luther Wesley Smith Discovers Green Lake

Our story now flashes back to the summer of 1944, when bombs rained on Europe and parents prayed for the safety of their sons in the armed services. In the lobby of Roger Williams Inn, at the newly acquired Northern Baptist Assembly at Green Lake, Wisconsin, a small group gathered for another kind of prayer, promising to each other and to God to ease some of the hurt of the times and to bring the denomination to new understandings of what it meant to be the people of God. The dedication service for the Assembly was brief, but it presaged a ministry which was to draw people from all over the world to seek "a closer walk with God."

If there was a dominating emotion in the hearts of those gathered, it was gratitude—gratitude born of the conviction, to paraphrase the words of Dr. C. Oscar Johnson, that "God has been preparing this place for Baptists for more than fifty years; it only remains for them to make it their own by completing the task of raising the money for purchase, and developing the program for which it is so admirably suited."

The period of preparation of which Dr. Johnson spoke had begun with a sudden summer storm in 1888, in which a boatload of vacationers found it necessary to take refuge in the shelter of the cove formed by what came to be called Lone Tree Point. The day had begun pleasantly enough, with Mrs. Victor Lawson, wife of a rising young Chicago newspaper publisher, renting a boat at the village of Green Lake for a pleasure cruise. Already the area was a favorite vacation spot for people like the Lawsons. Most of the lake's shoreline was owned by farmers, but access was easy, and the summer population of urbanites was in sharp contrast to the farmers and villagers who remained the year round. With the first sudden gusts of wind rippling the lake's surface, the captain ordered the vessel back to shore. Return to the dock was impossible; so he put into the cove, and the party struggled ashore. Huddled in a nearby shack, watching the elements churn the water and batter their boat, Mrs. Lawson resolved that one day she would return to purchase that very spot, and there establish a place of retreat from the struggles of the city which she and her friends called home.

THE LAWSON DREAM

In December of that year the dream began to become a reality. The Lawsons purchased ten acres of land, including the point, at a cost of $1,429. Adding farm to farm during the next few years, they increased the estate to 1100 acres, and a lovely house on the point became the focus of life for what was conceived as a "gentleman's farm." A barn was built for a herd of Jersey cattle, another for Guernseys, and yet another for bulls. There was a sheep barn, a hog house, and a horse barn. Building was on such a lavish scale that, although it was considered a working farm, it yielded no profit for its owners. But profit was not its purpose. Mrs. Lawson worked at its development as a hobby, and in so doing, some believed, participated in carrying out God's will, in order to fulfill the dream of another with far different purpose.

As the Lawson dream unfolded, a network of roads laced the fields and forests, connecting the two main sets of farm buildings and the residence with a series of water towers built (legend has it) at places where Mrs. Lawson's little donkey, Cadichon, stopped to rest while taking her on trips around the estate. The main tower rises more than two hundred feet above the surface of the lake. Equipped with a stairway, its observation platform provided the finest panoramic view of the lake and countryside anywhere in the area. Between the tower and the water is a greensward of several acres, reclaimed from its former swampy condition by building a retaining wall and filling behind it. Offshore an island was formed in the same way. Stone walls and bridges of pleasing design were constructed from the rocks worn round and deposited by the glaciers centuries before. Whatever the Lawsons did, they did well, using the best of planning and materials, so that most of what was built is still in use today. Because of her extensive travel, particularly in Europe, Mrs. Lawson was able to bring ideas from far and wide to enhance her Lone Tree Farm. Exotic flowers and trees were planted, and because of their protection from cattle grazing and logging, a number of native species were protected which otherwise have become difficult to find in that part of the state.

But the Lawson dream bubble burst in 1914 with the death of Mrs. Lawson, who had been the driving force behind the project for twenty-six years. When Victor Lawson died in 1925, the estate was sold to the H. O. Stone Company of Chicago. The gentleman's farm gave way to Lawsonia, a businessman's playground. Again development was on a grand scale and with good taste. The Lawson house was moved, and a luxury hotel of eighty-one rooms was built in its place. A swimming pool was constructed; a yacht basin was developed; and tennis courts and bridle paths were added to make the grounds attractive for recreation. The Lawsonia Country Club included one of the finest eighteen-hole golf courses in the Midwest. A part of the plan was to develop homesites for private owners, who became members of the organization and enjoyed the privileges of the grounds. Twenty-five such homes were built during the first few years of the Stone Company's development. While a few might be considered modest in design and cost, most of them were in keeping with the luxurious style of the Lawsons.

Many historical events depend upon timing for their significance. Had Victor Lawson also died in 1914, so that the Stone development could have taken place during the early 1920s, the grounds might have become completely and permanently the Lawsonia the developers envisioned. But the ¾ million dollars spent on the hotel and the three to four million dollars on other improvements were badly timed. October of 1929 saw the crash of the financial structure of the nation, and the Great Depression followed. Much of the funding for development was borrowed capital—dollars obtained when money was easy had to be repaid at depression levels of income. The property went in receivership, to be held by the Illinois Continental Bank and Trust Company of Chicago until 1943.

Though banks do not usually engage in the resort business, an effort was made to recoup the investment by continuing to operate on a modest scale. The lingering depression was followed by wartime gas rationing, so that even those with money to afford its luxury could not come to Green Lake. The buildings were closed, employees were dismissed, and the gates were locked. The dream was dead, or so it seemed. And well it might have been, had it not been God's dream, with the Lawsons and the Stone Company in reality serving as his instruments, unwittingly but nonetheless effectively.

FROM FOOL'S PARADISE TO PROMISED LAND

Luther Wesley Smith was a dreamer, too. He did not command the kind of financial resources available to the Lawsons, nor did he have in mind a paradise for the pleasure of a few. He was God's man at the right place at the right time to discover the Northern Baptist Assembly (renamed the American Baptist Assembly in 1951).

Smith had dreamed of a conference center where American Baptists might meet for instruction and inspiration. He saw such a center as a place of healing for the tensions which for many years had plagued the denomination. Wherever he went on denominational business, he had his private agenda, to find the right spot for the conference center he envisioned. In June, 1943, he visited the office of the Reverend David Witte, Director of Christian Education for the Wisconsin Baptist State Convention. As the two men drove across the state, Smith shared his dream for a national conference center. He concluded: "Surely in a great state like Wisconsin with all its beautiful lakes, there must be some place that could serve the purpose we have in mind." Witte declined any knowledge of such a place, then added as an afterthought: "Of course, there's that fool's paradise up at Green Lake, but for Baptists that would be out of the question."

That remark was enough for Dr. Smith. He insisted on knowing more, and in a matter of minutes the route of travel was altered toward Green Lake. The gates of Lawsonia were locked, but in typical style Smith convinced a caretaker that he ought to be let inside to tour the grounds. As the two men drove around, Dr. Smith's dream became a picture of the future: the barns would become dormitories and meeting halls, the hotel a place for more affluent guests; smaller buildings would provide classrooms, and recreational facilities would be adapted or provided. "This is it! We've got to have it." His mind was made up, and he went back to plan his strategy.

George Moll, Smith's business adviser, was asked to make discreet inquiries concerning the situation and report back. It was soon learned that the bank owned the property and would like to sell promptly in order to take a "tax loss," and that the most recent offer had been for $250,000. Discussions with bank officials followed. It was found that Baptist layman James L. Kraft, the cheese executive, was a court-appointed trustee of the bankrupt Lawsonia. Mr. Kraft and denominational officials entered the discussion, and on December 7, 1943, Luther Wesley Smith had his third meeting with Mr. Binny, the officer in charge of the Lawsonia mortgage. Of that meeting Dr. Smith reported:

> Once with Mr. Binny, I laid on his desk a bank check made out to his bank for $75,000.00 and indicated I was authorized to offer a purchase price of $300,000.
> Mr. Binny scowled and indicated that was not enough of an offer. At that point I launched into a spontaneous speech on the responsibility of the bank to sell not to a notorious gambling syndicate that was devoted to tearing down the character of the very young men who were at that moment dying on battlefields in Europe or indeed to some other organization which might perpetuate the demoralizing influences which the Lawsonia Country Club had wielded with its gambling casino and drinking bouts. Rather it was the responsibility of the bank to help put back into Wisconsin the moral character-building influences of religious faith and high ideals. After a heated several minutes, I said: "Mr. Binny, knowing what this bank has put into that property in dollars, the property's worth, knowing the other alternatives, I believe my Board considers this a fair offer and as good a one as we can defend with our constituency. Please call your officers together *now* and give them this offer. Our American Baptist Publication Society is the purchaser under the conditions you outlined. Here is your check."
> It was a long 12 to 13 minutes before he came back.
> "They accept your offer!" declared Mr. Binny.

When the purchase was complete, it was as though the children of Israel had come into the Promised Land. Luther Wesley Smith was the Moses who had dreamed the dream, and though unlike Moses he did enter it, his active career was brought to a tragic end with a severe heart attack in June, 1951, which made him an invalid for the remainder of his life. This did not come, however, before the dreamer had begun to see his dreams take shape in the transformation of buildings to house the program he envisioned and the trial years of conference development completed. The Assembly Board of Directors, at the time of Smith's retirement as Executive Secretary, recorded this tribute:

> It was not an easy task that Dr. Smith had set for himself. Even after the appropriate place was found, and became available, there were difficulties and barriers which were apparently insurmountable. Yet with unquenchable enthusiasm and resolute facing of every difficulty of whatever nature, he clung tenaciously to his idea. Always

there was the note of confident faith in the leading of God, and reliance upon His continuing guidance and blessing.

In the opening chapters of Genesis, God gave Adam the privilege of naming the creatures he had made. The giving of a name is a familiar way by which a person or a group lays claim to a city or to a new land. At the Assembly the land was possessed not only as buildings were put to new use, but as they came to be known by new names. A tour of the grounds is like tracing the names of Baptist and other Christian leaders across the pages of history:

The Lawsonia Hotel became the Roger Williams Inn, honoring the founder of First Baptist Church, Providence, Rhode Island, the first Baptist church in America.

The garage became Morehouse Hall, in memory of Henry R. Morehouse, who served as secretary of the American Baptist Home Mission Society for thirty-eight years.

The building once used to house the Lawsons' farm workers was named for Brayton Case, the preacher-farmer-missionary to Burma.

The Jersey barn was named John Clarke Lodge, after the first pastor of the First Baptist Church at Newport, Rhode Island, and, along with Roger Williams, founder of the state.

The bull barn became the Bruce Kinney Lodge in memory of the man who served for thirty-eight years as director of Indian work for the Home Mission Society.

The carriage house was given the name Rauschenbusch Hall, in honor of the well-known professor at Rochester Divinity School.

The name of Judson, commemorating the great missionary to Burma, was given to the Assembly's outstanding landmark, the main water tower.

The early Baptist educator and evangelist in Missouri and Illinois, John Mason Peck, was chosen to be remembered in the power house, cleared of its machinery and used first for administration, then for meeting rooms.

The Guernsey barn became William Carey Hall in the Abbey Area, in memory of the first Baptist missionary from England to India. This is the largest building on the grounds and had been used to house German prisoners of war at the time the Assembly was purchased.

What had been the root cellar became the Spurgeon Chapel, in honor of the famous London pastor and preacher.

John Frederic Oberlin, the Lutheran pastor from Alsace who provided untold inspiration to the leaders of the town and country church movement in America, is memorialized in Oberlin Lodge, once the hog barn for the Lawsons.

Seeking to make names appropriate to building use, the green-tiled pump house became the Albert Schweitzer Organ Studio, which now serves as a Bait and Tackle Shop.

One of the most inspiring spots on the entire grounds is the Cathedral in the Glen. This was constructed by high school youth as a replica of the outdoor chapel built by Baptist missionaries at Hopevale in the Philippines during the Japanese occupation in World War II, where eleven missionaries were killed. The quiet walk to this memorial is marked by verses written by Jennie A. Adams, who was among the martyred.

USING THE LAND TO FULFILL GOD'S DREAM

It is the nature of dreams to require concrete expression if they are to touch the life of the world. Acquisition of the Lawson estate was vital to this process, but it was not an end in itself. Dr. Smith had no notion that the mere purchase of real estate would meet the needs of the denomination. In keeping with the envisioned educational nature of the program, the Assembly would be administratively related to the Board of Education and Publication, but would be given direction by its own representative Board of Directors. At its first meeting on February 4, 1944, J. C. Clark was appointed business manager. It was expected that denominational agencies would provide program, while the Assembly furnished the meeting place and facilities. As Mr. Clark began to assemble the needed staff, he found that many of the former employees of the Lawsons and the subsequent management lived in the vicinity and were pleased to return to work. Students and retired persons, eager for the experience of working in such a setting at a modest remuneration, supplemented the full-time work force.

With the Assembly providing facility management, the Baptist Youth Fellowship became the first to meet at Green Lake. The youth conference in June, 1944, had more than three hundred in attendance. Dr. Weldon M. Wilson, pastor of North Shore Baptist Church, conducted inauguration ceremonies. Next came American Baptist Men, who climaxed their conference with a decision to assume responsibility for raising the funds to pay for the property. John A. Dawson, an investment counselor in Chicago, was selected to guide the project. His leadership and the support of the men of the denomination were significant factors in carrying the task to its conclusion. He was later to become president of the Convention.

The first season closed on September 4, after a total of 3,150 persons had participated in nine conferences. They went home enthusiastic about the Assembly as a place for summer growth opportunities. But others extended the dream. Beginning in 1945, the American Baptist Home Mission Societies, under the leadership of Dr. Mark Rich, sponsored in-service schools for ministers of town and country fields during the winter months. A Rural Church Center was established, with offices in Shepherds Lodge, the former sheep barn. During the first fifteen years nearly a thousand pastors received field-oriented training in these schools. Under the leadership of the Reverend Robert Frerichs, the center came to serve urban

143

needs as well during the 1960s. Here many new concepts of ministry were studied and field tested, and later applied to the larger church.

During the second year of operation the Children's Center was inaugurated under the leadership of Dr. Pearl Rosser. Miss Lois Blankenship, after whom it was later named, became the director in its second season. Organized particularly for the training of workers with children, the center fostered some of the most progressive ideas in Christian education found anywhere. Experimentation with new methods was undertaken. New architectural designs were developed to fulfill educational needs. Many church committees have found the Children's Center buildings creative models for their own construction of educational facilities. The nursery building, constructed in 1964, is an outstanding example of architecture subservient to programming function.

What happened in ministry with children and with rural ministers occurred also in many other departments of American Baptist life. A glance at the 1958 program schedule shows that the Assembly, after fifteen years, had reached a stage of stability and viability. It had become an integral part of American Baptist life.

The Seminary Middlers' Conference, a place of fellowship and understanding of the denomination and its leadership. About 300 future pastors and leaders and their wives or husbands attended these annual conferences sponsored by the various agencies of the denomination.

The National Student Conference. More than 500 participated that year.

The Conference on Christian Higher Education, for college and seminary presidents, student workers, deans, and public relations personnel.

The Christian Writers' Conference, devoted to creative writing for church publications.

The Children's Center, where boys and girls "become engaged in learning about" the Christian life under the supervision of teachers gathered from across the country to improve their skills in Christian education.

The Radio and Television Workshop, where the heat of klieg lights and notices of "On the air" were indicators that those interested in the field of broadcasting were hard at work.

The National Laymen's Conference, a time of sharing ideas about men's work, the communication of the gospel and the support of the church at home and abroad. The first fifteen years saw 7,000 men participating.

The National Women's Conference. (In 1972 and again in 1973 American Baptist Men and American Baptist Women held their conferences cooperatively.)

The Conference on Christian Social Concern, studying problems of injustice and oppression, and appropriate Christian responses were planned.

The Conference on Worship and the Arts for developing talents to help lead men and women and young people to God.

The National Missions' Conference, a stirring reminder of Baptist commitment of the preaching of Christ to all people. The Avenue of Flags above the rose garden is a constant witness to this dedication.

The National Ministers' Conference, a means of rediscovering the power of prayer and the Bible for many. In the first fifteen years an aggregate of more than 6,000 ministers and their spouses were enriched by this closer walk with God.

The National Young Adult Family Camps, a period of "togetherness" as families used the extensive camping facilities on the Assembly grounds.

The Recreation Leaders' Lab, where skills for meaningful play were learned to take back home.

The National Christian Education Workers' Conference, where conferees learned the utilization of group dynamics for a better church school program. Participation topped 500 each year.

The Evangelism and Bible Conference, a period of careful planning to help churches prepare for their ministry.

The 1958 schedule showed seventeen major Baptist conferences. These plus numerous other gatherings and several non-Baptist sessions added up to a very busy year at the Assembly. A staff of more than four hundred persons served the needs of guests as they added their labor to the dreams of Luther Wesley Smith.

Planners like Richard Hoiland and financial supporters like James L. Kraft, John A. Dawson, Omer E. Robbins, Harry L. Jenkins, and George Moll made their unique contributions. During the period from 1944 to 1952 J. C. Clark guided the Assembly through the creation of its organization and its development as a viable system. Under Grant Anderson's executive leadership from 1952 to 1959 the Assembly gained stability and was on its way to becoming accepted not only among Baptists, but among others as well. Major accomplishments of the first fifteen years included alteration of buildings to meet growing program needs. The number of groups sponsoring conferences and the number of persons attending grew steadily. Administration developed to a high level of efficiency.

Dr. J. E. Dollar became resident director in 1959, and during his first ten years of administration contributed to increased stability and the gaining of a significant reputation. In a part of the country where the population is overwhelmingly Lutheran or Roman Catholic, the very presence of the Assembly was cause for surprise to many local residents in the early years. They could not believe that Baptists were strong enough to own and operate such a facility. But the Assembly's presence became accepted, and gradually its ecumenical hosting possibilities were recognized as well.

At first small retreat groups began to request time on the schedule. As it became known that the facilities were available, local churches, synods, and other regional church groups, many of them Lutheran, looked to Green Lake as their meeting place, especially during the fall, winter, and spring seasons, which are conducive to short time spans, short travel distances, and therefore to use by local and regional groups. With rising costs for operation it became increasingly important that the facilities be winterized to make them usable year round. Scheduling of more than one conference at a time became desirable in order to get maximum use out of the facilities.

Dr. Dollar's openness to this ecumenical style soon led to the addition of many character-building and educational conferences on the Assembly's schedule. Wisconsin groups, such as the Future Farmers of America and the Governor's Conference on Business Development, chose the Assembly as a meeting place. The Assembly gradually changed from a strictly Baptist center to a diversity of uses for the broadest possible service to mankind.

Because of multiple programming, larger dining and meeting rooms were needed. The Lakeview Dining Room and Pillsbury Hall were built in 1956 to supplement the Crystal Room and Morehouse Hall. In order to place administration more nearly in the center of activities, the first unit of the Kraft Administration building was constructed in 1963. The second unit was added in 1966. At the Children's Center the nursery building was dedicated in 1967, completing the facilities for that popular aspect of conference ministry. The building commemorating Baptist World Missions was completed in 1966, and dedication took place the following year. The only major housing-conference facility constructed by the Assembly, Lieder Haus, was completed in 1970. It is a self-contained building, with sleeping and conference rooms, adjacent to the Children's Center, and close enough to the General Conference Area to utilize its dining and other facilities. In the Abbey Area, Oberlin Lodge was rebuilt and improved after a fire partially destroyed it in 1968, and major improvement of rooms was undertaken in the west wing of William Carey Hall.

The trend toward service to outside groups was not met with universal pleasure. While for many, including staff and Board, broader use was significant of a theological point of view which accepted ecumenicity on the one hand and cooperation with other nonprofit organizations on the other, some began to raise questions about use of the Assembly for other than Baptist groups. Still others raised serious questions about the concept of the Assembly as primarily a "facilities management" organization.

In order to determine the future direction for Board and staff, a

146

two-year study was authorized under the guidance of the Program Advisory Committee. The end of the study was to coincide with the close of twenty-five years of ministry at Green Lake, and it provided the basis for planning a transition into the organizational phase known as "maturity." During this period, one looks for development of uniqueness on the part of the organization and of increased adaptability. Life was to be concerned with the development of self-identity to a new degree and the adoption of a stance that permitted a more flexible response to new movements and changed needs.

NEW PROGRAM THRUST

The celebration of the Assembly's twenty-fifth anniversary in 1968 was more than the recognition of a quarter century of service to American Baptists. It was the beginning of a new thrust in program development which was designed to set the tone for the next quarter century. Although public seminars were held to study emerging trends, a major anniversary accomplishment emerged quietly in the Board of Directors.

The Board's Program Advisory Committee, under the chairmanship of Dr. Dorothy Bucklin, presented its study findings in 1968. Dr. Harvey A. Everett had been commissioned in 1967 to help the committee determine American Baptist needs which could be met at the Assembly. Extensive interviews with educational consultants, conference planners, denominational executives, and lay/clergy leaders yielded a wealth of information. The resulting study report projected the need for building upon the heritage of national conferences with more emphasis upon the Assembly's unique opportunity for its own program development. The implication was that facilities management would be guided by program needs. Although the report called for a Director of Facilities and a Director of Program with equal status, the Board decided to take a transition step by adding a full-time Program Director to the Assembly's administrative staff, leaving primary responsibility for facilities development with the Resident Director.

The title of Program Director has been used previously to refer to the Educational Ministries' staff person from the national offices in Valley Forge who spent the summer at Green Lake as a conference services' coordinator. Administratively he was responsible to the Executive Secretary of the Board of Education and Publication. The contributions of Dr. Richard Hoiland, Dr. Clarence Gilbert, and Dr.

Joseph John Hanson provided an enviable record of achievement. Under the new plan, however, year-round residence was to be established at Green Lake, with primary administrative responsibility to the Assembly administrator.

Dr. William R. Nelson became the first full-time Program Director in the summer of 1970. His presence personified the commitment that had been made by the Board of Directors in 1968:

> that the role of a national conference center, such as the American Baptist Assembly, must be considered within the broader framework of the total denominational strategy for leader development (both lay and clergy without distinction) and conversely that the continued ownership and operation of the facility including any further development of its accommodations be a response to clearly discovered program needs revealed within that total strategy, and not *vice versa.*

Although Dr. Nelson supplemented the ongoing national conferences planned in Valley Forge with more Assembly-sponsored programming, his main contribution as Program Director was in relation to comprehensive master planning in response to program trends. The foundational Study Report of 1968 was followed by a Green Lake "Think Tank" in May, 1972. The architectural firm known as Dimensional Dynamics of Valley Forge was requested to plan and implement a process aimed at isolating a variety of program trends that should guide facility development for the next ten years. The thirteen persons who met at the Valley Forge Hilton consisted of a representative group of educational consultants, denominational executives, conference planners, and lay/clergy leaders. In addition to extensive data gathering during the "Think Tank" experience, there was a careful follow-up period of data processing. The result was a comprehensive master-planning process report from Dimensional Dynamics which met with a favorable response from the Board of Directors in August. This report firmly established four priorities for facility development in response to program needs:

1. A Family Camping Program was authorized immediately and was in operation during the summer of 1973. The new cluster concept of programming is related to a year-round Activity Center. Campsites are arranged in circles of twelve, with a utility building in the center of each circle. Capital outlay, including cost of needed roads and utility lines, amounted to $150,000. Recent Baptist history was acknowledged by naming the multipurpose Activity Center for Dr. C. Oscar Johnson, former pastor of the Third Baptist Church, St. Louis. His earlier interest in developing Green Lake as a family

enrichment center is symbolized by the four St. Louis cottages which are adjacent to the Johnson Activity Center.

2. Planning began immediately for the Luther Wesley Smith Center, a remodeling and expansion of the major conference complex in honor of the Assembly's founder. Dr. Smith's death in 1971 reminded many people of the need to establish a fitting memorial to his creative leadership at Green Lake. An earlier plan to erect a separate chapel-meeting hall was abandoned in favor of upgrading the present Pillsbury Hall, Lakeview Dining Room, and Roger Williams Inn complex according to current program needs. The approval of this plan marked the beginning of the second major development program in the Assembly's history. The memory of Luther Wesley Smith will be perpetuated throughout this major conference complex, which represents both the fulfillment of his last dream and the heart of the present program emphasis.

3. A clergy center for continuing education was projected as a future program need. Although the former ministry of the Rural and Urban Church Center was phased out in 1968, consideration is being given again to the kind of support ministry for clergy which could be carried out in a setting like Green Lake. A Task Force on Professional Clergy Development began meeting in the spring of 1973 in order to determine the kind of programming which would be most appropriate for such a center.

4. Another need which was projected in the 1972 comprehensive master plan is a Chautauqua program in the Abbey Area. The ideal atmosphere in the "hayloft" of William Carey Hall could provide the setting for creative programming in drama and music. Utilization of this converted barn for such events is presently a regular feature of the Church Musicians' Conference, especially the annual recital on the three-manual Allen Organ.

When Dr. J. E. Dollar retired as Resident Director at the end of 1972, the Board of Directors took another step toward implementing the 1968 Study Report. They asked Dr. Nelson to become the Executive Director, a title change which recognized the increased status of the Assembly within the life of the total denomination. The new Program Director, who joined the Assembly staff early in 1973, was the Reverend Lawrence H. Janssen. His eighteen-year background with the American Baptist Home Mission Societies added a new dimension of credibility and experience to the growing program emphasis. In addition he was given responsibility for handling promotion. The Reverend B. R. Pfaff, from the Ministers and Missionaries Benefit Board, joined the Assembly's administrative staff during the summer of 1973 in the new position of Associate Director—Finance and Development. Mr. Janssen's title was changed at the same time to Associate Director—Program and Promotion, in recognition of his actual responsibilities. The interagency background of these new staff members reflects the Assembly's growing awareness of its conference ministry to the entire denomination.

The past thirty years at Green Lake have added a resounding "Yes" to the initial inquiry that was made by Dr. Smith and others during the uncertain wartorn time of decision in 1943. The extent of their vision can be measured quite accurately now by the reality of the results. Dr Richard Hoiland said: "There are many in our denomination who insist that the crowning achievement of Luther's illustrious career was the founding of the American Baptist Assembly at Green Lake, Wisconsin, which has come to be recognized as probably the foremost religious conference center in America, if not in the world."

can Baptist Assembly,
Lake, Wisconsin

8. Expanding *the Witness*

New Advances in Christian Education and Publication

Our setting shifts to New York City in the summer of 1898. It was hot as usual, and the streets were teeming with people—adults, young people, and children. It was particularly the latter group which concerned Mrs. Walker Aylett Hawes, a physician's wife who was superintendent of the children's department of the Sunday school at the Epiphany Baptist Church (later, a constituent part of Calvary Baptist Church). Mrs. Hawes was deeply concerned about the children of the East Side, a densely populated area about a mile from the church, where the children played unsupervised in the busy and dangerous streets, and often got into trouble. There ought to be a better way, thought Mrs. Hawes, remembering her far different childhood in Charlottesville, Virginia.

Encouraged by her pastor, Dr. Howard Lee Jones, she struggled with the problem until an answer began to come. She would have a "vacation" school. There would be a time of worship and a time for Bible stories. There would be singing and games. Arts and crafts suitable for boys and girls would be taught. It would all be fun. It would be Christian education. It would be evangelism. It would be social service. She walked the streets looking for a place. There seemed to be none.

153

Finally, Mrs. Hawes saw a possibility. She must have been desperate, for this was a beer garden! The owner rented the place at 324 East 71st Street to her for six weeks' daytime use at a cost of twenty-five dollars a month. She was in business, the vacation church school business.

VACATION CHURCH SCHOOLS

At first, this new school received scant attention. One newspaper, the *Commercial Advertiser,* carried a story on July 27, 1898, terming the endeavor a "novel enterprise of the Reverend Howard Lee Jones." Miss Theodosia N. Hazen, a helper in the early days, recalled many years later, "I will never forget the old drunks who came out of the saloon and hung on the gate to the beer garden to hear the children sing their sweet Christian songs; and my, how those children could sing." All this was ignored by church leaders until early in 1901 when Dr. Robert G. Boville came to preach one Sunday at the Epiphany Church.

As the newly elected executive of the New York Baptist City Mission Society, Dr. Boville was on the alert for ways and means to meet the growing challenge of the urban situation. He learned of the vacation school project and quickly sensed its rightness. Moving swiftly, he prepared recommendations for support and expansion of Mrs. Hawes' endeavor. Five daily vacation Bible schools were planned. Each would be aided by a student from the Union Theological Seminary across the city. One of these five young seminarians was Harry Emerson Fosdick, later to be pastor of the famed Riverside Church and a professor at Union. It was his springboard into active Christian service. He once remarked that he had had "a marvelous summer."

Apparently, the whole project was so rewarding that the next year the Mission Society sponsored ten schools, and in 1903 there were seventeen! By now, curriculum was a growing concern, so Dr. Boville prepared the Bible studies. Mrs. L. P. J. Bishop, of the Women's Auxiliary of the Society, prepared the material for arts and crafts. Dr. William H. Sears, of Columbia University, arranged "the marching exercises and the physical training activities" and the games.

The Reverend Charles H. Sears and the Reverend Albert H. Gage were also among those involved. Evidently they learned as well as they taught, for Sears later served for thirty-seven years as the executive secretary of the New York Baptist Mission Society, and

Gage became an honored minister and author of practical books on Christian education and pastoral theology. Dr. Boville became so enamored of the vacation school idea that he devoted the remainder of his life to the movement. He was, at his death in 1937, affiliated with the World Association of Vacation Bible Schools, an organization he had founded fifteen years before.

Naturally, such a burgeoning movement as the vacation church school would spread. It did spread, among other places, to Philadelphia, where an energetic and talented young lady named Elizabeth M. Finn became involved. One summer Mrs. Finn and some helpers raised a tent on a vacant lot in a residential section of the city and conducted a summer vacation Bible school. It was such a success that later a church was organized and an attractive edifice erected. The Overbrook Baptist Church gives continuing witness to the influence of this vacation school. Mrs. Finn became director of the Department of Vacation and Weekday Church Schools for American Baptists, serving until 1949.

Long before, in 1915, the Publication Society had accepted responsibility of vacation schools, including promotion and curriculum publication. The first book published as a vacation school text by the Society was *Dan of Nazareth*. It appeared in 1918 as an ungraded book without handwork suggestions. By 1920, however, the Society began publishing a cycle of eight books graded for beginners, primary and junior children. By 1925 a cycle of three intermediate (junior high) rural and urban texts was begun.

Churches began to see the great opportunities offered by the vacation schools and, prompted by earnest pastors and the active leadership offered by the Society, started to sponsor these summertime activities on a wide scale. In 1923, 721 schools were listed by American Baptist churches in states from Maine to California. Riding a growth curve, this total reached 3759 in 1941.

All this was demanding more and better materials from the publishing house and these were provided. It was at this time that there came forth from the presses the popular *Jesus, Our Friend,* by Elizabeth Shields; *Learning More About God,* by Louise S. Linder; *Worshipping God,* by Grace Smetzer; and *Jesus, the Great Leader,* by Mae Deal Shane and Irene A. Jones.

New days and new times brought, of course, new situations demanding new means. Many churches found it advantageous to cooperate with other churches in the community for the vacation

155

school project. This fact together with the high cost of producing materials led the Society to engage in the cooperative publication of texts and teachers' guides. The increasing use of the automobile and the growing affluence of society caused a great mobility among the people during vacation time. For these causes, and numerous others, the vacation church school adopted different models to fit particular situations. During the 1950s and the 1960s about two thousand American Baptist churches normally held some kind of vacation school.

CAMPS, CONFERENCES, AND ASSEMBLIES

Another summertime effort which arose among the churches in the early part of the twentieth century was the camp and conference movement. The modest attention this received from the Society was greatly accelerated when, in 1945, a camp and assembly department was established. Called to lead this work was Rev. Rodney Britten, director of Christian education for the Oregon Baptist State Convention. He remained in the post some twenty-five years and was instrumental in making many changes across the American Baptist landscape.

In 1922 the Publication Society listed twenty-six summer assemblies. Not every state convention sponsored such activities, but there was a wide distribution. At least thirteen of these assemblies were on college or prep school campuses. By 1946, however, Mr. Britten could report that "almost every state" in the Convention was moving into outdoor education and planning a camp expansion program. The shift in emphasis from assemblies to camps was significant in that it reflected a new stress on informal learning in a natural setting where campers lived in small groups and made discoveries about God, nature, and human relationships. In due course Mr. Britten could also report that a handbook on architecture had been written as a guide in camp construction for the many areas that were developing new campsites. A new curriculum had been prepared which included: *God's Plan for Life* (Juniors), *Adventuring Together as Christians* (Junior High), and *Discipleship with Christ* (Senior High). Within a year these courses had been expanded to a complete three-year cycle of graded materials with an added program for family camping. By then over 50,000 persons were sharing in these summer activities conducted in 125 Baptist camps.

The upward movement continued throughout the 1950s. The

Typical scene at a Baptist
Camp

eeting of national Baptist Youth Fellowship officers

157

various state conventions struggled valiantly with the growing costs of site development and maintenance. Leadership was always a problem. Pastors usually were called upon to serve as teachers and directors, but this practice had numerous built-in limitations. Although some agreed to release their pastors for camp duties, others insisted on calling such camp duties vacation time. A two-week stint at a Baptist camp could hardly be considered a vacation! It was soon discovered, too, that year-round leadership was demanded for promotion, program planning, direction of maintenance, and fund raising. No longer was camping simply a matter of finding a place to pitch a few tents and build a campfire. Permanent and valuable buildings were being erected, and churches were beginning to use the camps for winter weekend retreats and for major conferences.

Outdoor education had become an accepted part of the Christian movement. In some cases, the camp staff and budget almost equaled those of the state conventions. The intensive period of time involved, the close associations established, and the opportunities for personal development were values not to be cast aside. Thousands of youth found Christ as their Savior in Baptist camps; many others dedicated their lives to professional Christian service there. But this success only increased the problems. Seeking reasonable solutions, some areas began to work cooperatively with other denominations. What was found to be too much for one group of churches to carry might be borne by two or more working together. The rapid growth of urban development added to the problem of camp development also. Land once deemed isolated enough for the "outdoors" and "retreat" concepts was often found to be suddenly surrounded by homesites.

None of this, of course, could remove the memories of joy and wonder that campers carried with them as they returned to their homes and their churches. Whenever they gathered to reminisce or to give more prosaic reports to some congregation or Sunday school class that had sponsored their attendance, the comic as well as the serious was sure to be a part of the story. One pastor, for instance, can never forget his experience in one vesper service while preaching in a lovely evergreen cathedral beside a lake. At the close of worship, he gave an invitation to the assembled youth to receive Christ, if they had not already done so, or to dedicate themselves to the Master wherever he should lead. It was not the decision of any that night to so respond, but that lack was hardly attributable either to the resistance of the youth or to the ineptness of the preacher. For to the surprise of the latter and the glee of the former, promptly upon the issuance of the invitation, several full-bodied, white-downed ducks came sedately waddling down the pine-scented aisle! They were among friends; and the preacher had often fed them. To his familiar voice they responded. Such learning experiences—and who knows what the youth made of this?—were the very warp and woof of Christian camp life.

Not all vesper services ended like that, to be sure. Indeed, it could be reported in 1948 that over four thousand young people were converted to the Christian faith in Baptist camps that summer. Thus, one more means of multiplying the witness had been found.

BAPTIST LEADER

One of the first major changes made by Luther Wesley Smith upon his becoming executive secretary of the Publication Society was in Sunday school publications. For many years, three group magazines had been produced—*Children's Leader, Young People's Leader,* and *Adult Leader.* These had served the churches well; but, based upon the findings of Henry E. Cole, Leonard R. Jenkins, and the curriculum committee, Dr. Smith directed that these three magazines be combined into one. A new format was chosen and publication of *Baptist Leader* began in the spring of 1939.

It was a substantial journal of 64 pages, designed to serve a broad spectrum of reader interest. In addition to major divisions directed to workers with children, youth, and adults, there were also timely articles on more general religious topics, book reviews, Baptist news, and other items. The art work was carefully chosen, and generous space was given to photographs. Pastors and concerned lay folk in the churches soon made extensive use of *Baptist Leader.*

In the first issue for January, 1940, for instance, one finds such articles as the following: "New Testament Manuscripts," by Dean Ernest C. Colwell, of the Divinity School at the University of Chicago; a stirring piece on "The Truth about Intoxicants"; and a pertinent and encouraging story on the Calvary Baptist Church, Washington, D.C., "Can a Church Grow in the Heart of a Big City?"

One also learns that the new post office at O'Fallon, Illinois, was decorated with a beautiful mural on the life of the pioneer Baptist, John Mason Peck. The accompanying story reviewed the salient features of Peck's life, including the fact that he once served as a postmaster nearby!

Reading on, one learns that the Illinois Baptist State Convention had moved its headquarters from Bloomington to Springfield; that the Reverend Dr. Angelo Di Domenica had just celebrated his twenty-fifth anniversary as pastor of the First Italian Baptist Church of Philadelphia; and that the South Dakota Baptist Convention had taken, as one of its goals for the following year, an increased circulation of 2,000 copies of *The Secret Place* among its members. Perhaps these items were not of earth-shaking consequence, but they are the stuff of normal church life. The *Baptist Leader* supplied this information along with full material on the Sunday school lessons. With regular writers, such as seminary professors J. W. Bailey and L. Earl Jackson, prominent pastors Howard K. Williams and Bernard C. Clausen, and such talented authors as Colena M. Anderson, how could one go wrong? The *Leader* was enthusiastically received from the first and rightly so. It was the "most ambitious church periodical of the kind" ever undertaken by the Society.

At first, circulation was a worry. It was estimated that this figure should reach 50,000 for a break-even point to be achieved. Since very few religious journals had ever gained such heights on a subscription basis, the editors were not thinking small. By 1951, however, they reported this figure to the Convention. Four years later, Dr. Benjamin P. Browne enthusiastically turned in a figure exceeding 70,000. This, by 1959, reached 75,000. "On the basis of the rule of the thumb of four persons to a magazine," said Dr. Browne, "that means that nearly 300,000 Baptists read the *Baptist Leader.*" It was a journalistic force with which to reckon. Its promotion of various denominational causes and programs was vitally important. Its noncontroversial nature was a healing and helping element among American Baptists to no small degree. It continues to be published today as a valued resource for Sunday church school teachers.

THE SECRET PLACE

Another publication which the Society found to hold a unique place among its constituency was the devotional booklet *The Secret Place.* It was already an established work with a circulation of 12,000 when the Publication Society assumed responsibility for it in 1939. The renewed interest was most apparent, for within a year the circulation reached 135,000. With a suggested Bible reading, a devotional paragraph prepared by some pastor or earnest lay person, and a brief prayer, the reader could move daily page by page through a regular routine of spiritual aid. The various authors submitted their material voluntarily or by the editor's invitation without recompense. By 1941, circulation was approximately 200,000.

The Secret Place was put to many uses. Pastors distributed it when making calls. It was popular with shut-ins. Thousands of families used it to direct thought and feeling at mealtime worship. As the nation moved into the war experience, the booklet was in great demand by chaplains and by Christian service personnel away from home. "Its circulation," the editor could write in 1947, "is larger than any other publication in the history of the Society." Eight years later, *The Secret Place* was reaching the astounding circulation of 450,000 copies. In spite of this remarkable figure, the circulation continued to rise and finally peaked at a half million. Even in the worldly 1970s it remains around 300,000.

Its publication is a cooperative effort by American Baptists and the Disciples of Christ, and its use is officially sponsored by the Canadian Baptists as well. One unusual feature is the regular publication of an edition in standard English Braille. This project is supported by special contributions and is sent without charge to the blind and to schools and libraries.

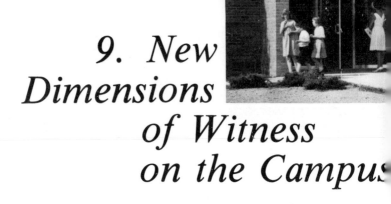

Baptist Student
Foundation at
Purdue University

9. New Dimensions of Witness on the Campus

Response
to
Changing
Needs
and
Patterns
in
Higher
Education

Christians in general and Baptists in particular have always been concerned about higher education. The numerous colleges and seminaries established by Baptist people and sacrificially supported by Baptist gifts attest to that fact. In return, the institutions are expected by the denomination to give good academic training, to provide an added dimension of Christian nurture, to help the graduates fulfill their calling not only in their own chosen fields of endeavor but also in the local church, and to give professional training for pastors, missionaries, and other workers in Christian education. So observed Dr. W. W. Charters, of Stephens College, Columbia, Missouri, a long-time member of the American Baptist Board of Education.

BAPTIST AUTONOMY

Several problems were inherent, however, in the fulfillment of these worthy goals. There was, first of all, the principle of Baptist autonomy, by which every church is an independent, self-governing, and complete entity, cooperating with other churches or religious organizations only insofar as it chooses. That Baptist schools of higher education took the same turn in the road, even to complete separation from the parent body, was not amazing. Faced with a choice between nonsectarianism and a denominational relationship that provided only a small fraction of needed financial support, many chose the former. The churches, in turn, reduced the flow of students as well as of what financial support there was.

It was to stem these tides of separatism that the Board of Education was organized. Its success was mixed. In 1914, shortly after its organization, the Board operated on a budget of $1,750. This meager sum gave little opportunity for program support or development. Five years later, however, the amount was $52,000. The next year, the budget climbed to $184,000, which supplied enough funds to at least "do something." The skyrocketing direction continued in 1921, when the Board had over one-half million dollars with which to work, and it reached its zenith in 1924 with the remarkable sum of $1,664,000! This, to be sure, was the result of special effort in the New World Movement, but many lean years were to follow. By the early 1940s it was time to appraise the situation once more.

THE HARTSHORNE-FROYD REPORT

Assigned to the project to survey the theological seminary scene were Dr. Hugh Hartshorne and Dr. Milton C. Froyd. This remarkably efficient team produced a report of far-reaching implications. They ascertained that only 36 percent of the ministers had received the recommended four years of college and three years of seminary education. Ten percent had no training beyond high school and 22 percent had been trained in short-term Bible schools which offered neither a liberal arts nor a graduate theological school curriculum. The fact that many of those who had not followed the recommended education route were achieving marked results for the Lord and that some who had done so were failures was beside the point. The circumstance was that the denomination was not in control of its professional leadership training.

To give direction to this study (the most intensive of its kind ever made by Baptists), Hartshorne and Froyd asked four basic questions:

1. What is the job of the minister?
2. Who are the candidates for the ministry?
3. How are candidates being trained?
4. What is the possible development of theological education among American Baptists?

In answering the initial question, they drew upon historical backgrounds. They noted that early Baptists had been moved, primarily, by a "concern for people," with ecclesiastical concerns taking second place. With this emphasis on the laity, the position of the clergy in those days was a low one, whose ordination was valid only for the ordaining church. In fact, some Baptists even felt that all baptized persons should be ordained. Practical considerations, however, prevailed by the nineteenth century as ordination became specialized and distinction between clergy and laity was made. The ministry, among Baptists, thus came to be perceived as *both* a calling and a profession.

Moving into contemporary times, Hartshorne and Froyd inquired as to what ministers and church leaders considered the responsibilities of the local church and the role of the clergy to be. The top items as listed by ninety-four churches then seeking a pastor were: in personal qualities he must be a "good mixer" and "sociable and agreeable"; in spiritual qualities, he must be "devoted to Christian calling and service to God" and "evangelistic"; as to leadership qualities, he should be "skilled in teaching and leading children and youth" and "skilled in preaching and teaching the gospel." The authors also reviewed the minister's use of time, his felt difficulties, and his sensitivity and response to community problems. These factors were thrown into juxtaposition with the educational preparation of the ministers to ascertain trends, strengths, and deficiencies.

The second major question probed the social and religious backgrounds of the theological students. To the surprise of some, it was discovered that although more than two-thirds of American Baptist churches were in small or rural communities, these by no means contributed their share of ministerial candidates. The "farmer boy to preacher man" cycle was being broken.

The investigators also inquired as to reasons for entering the ministry. The largest number, 44 percent, cited a "sense of call." That 66 percent of the students did not so respond would have surely surprised their Baptist ancestors. That only 17 percent of students in the newer seminaries and a mere 5 percent in the older seminaries had entered the ministry because of the need of men and society for Christ would have shocked them even more. That these levels were far higher than for those in seminaries of other denominations would not have been much consolation.

In answering the third question, the study led directly to the character of theological education and turned the spotlight on the seminaries themselves. Hartshorne and Froyd concluded that "the needs of the students for information and guidance are not adequately represented. There is almost no research going on regarding the job of the church, the problems of human conduct, the techniques of leadership and counselling, even in the age-old task of preaching." This was strong medicine, but there was more. The investigators added, "It is either taken for granted that all is known that needs to be known or there is lacking in the faculty the necessary skills for research in these neglected areas of church life and human need." In spite of generally limited budgets and overworked professors, it was clearly time for the seminaries to take remedial action.

In dealing with the final question, the study team made several recommendations. They suggested that the presidents of the seminaries, some Board of Education people, and other appropriate personnel be formed into a theological advisory committee to accomplish some cohesion and some sharing of aims and obstacles. From this general committee other task groups might be formed as follows: recruitment, ordination standards, field work for students, seminary curriculum, religious education in the seminaries, the relation between the colleges and the graduate theological schools, in-service training for ministers, the rural ministry, research in the professional activities of clergymen, and the relationship of the churches to the seminaries.

From this watershed of ideas there flowed in the years to follow a number of streams of denominational thought and action. The Hartshorne-Froyd report must be considered as one of the most far-reaching, and least controversial, that ever arose among American Baptists. Directly and indirectly, it brought many positive results. In 1950 the Commission on the Ministry was formed upon recommendation of the Committee of Review. From this came the Continuing Education program, first headed by Dr. Mark Rich. Later came the Center for the Ministry, established at Wellesley, Massachusetts. Making use of the best techniques in counseling and career guidance, pastors and their wives were, for a change, being placed on the receiving end of help. Other ways of assisting were developed. For instance, in 1968, guidance sessions with 220 pastors in California, Washington, Iowa, Oregon, and Kansas were held. A report on the ways ministers view their needs was made a basis of these interviews.

The theological conferences first held at Green Lake in 1954 were a strong feature of American Baptist life and prophetic of new insights and new confrontations in the area of Christian thought. Among the stream of study papers generated by the theological conferences are those which appeared in the Judson Press books *Baptist Concepts of the Church* and *Great Themes in Theology.*

Foundations, a Baptist journal of history and theology published quarterly, was introduced in January, 1958, by the American Baptist Historical Society with the support and encouragement of the Advisory Board for Theological Studies.

In 1961 the Convention adopted as a standard requirement for ordination the educational course of four years of college and three years of seminary. The denomination was still not ready to adopt much in the nature of theological guidelines or areas of professional competence for its clergy, but it was serious in establishing some direction and was willing to offer some aid to those called to be its servants.

Thus it was that in 1968 Dr. Lynn Leavenworth, director of the department of theological education, could list a full catalog of activities for the year, many of which had their beginning with the study report. Union had been established between Colgate Rochester Divinity School and Bexley Hall, an Episcopal seminary from Ohio. Crozer Seminary would join later. A cooperative plan for California Seminary and Berkeley Baptist Divinity School had been approved. In New England, Andover Newton Theological School, itself the product of a merger, had been one of the prime movers in the formation of the Theological Institute of Boston, which included leading schools of the area.

ESTABLISHING A FINANCIAL BASE

On a much wider educational front, American Baptists opened another attack in the late 1950s. This was a major capital fund-raising campaign for Christian higher education, both liberal arts and theological, known as the Christian Higher Education Challenge (CHEC). Under the direction of the Division of Christian Higher Education (Dr. Ronald V. Wells, director) the entire denomination was marshaled for the effort. With typical efficiency the firm of Marts and Lundy, which had served Baptists in other like campaigns, outlined strategy and ordered action.

The approach was the active enlistment of every church for

support. At the close of 1959, the first full year of the endeavor, some 1,199 churches had either raised or pledged $4,539,000, and ultimately $6,100,000 was received toward the goal of $7,500,000. Although naturally there was disappointment at not attaining 100 percent of the objective, this was the largest fund American Baptists had ever raised for the support of higher education. It was a worthy sum and aided many schools and student centers. Furthermore, it was a change from some financial drives in the past for higher education in that thousands of churches and many thousands of individuals were involved. Also, the need was made clear, and thus some individuals and churches were motivated to continue their support in other ways.

Another financial plan with wide-ranging effect was the National Scholarship Program. During the New Development Program of the Board of Education, a small fund for educational aid to the youth of American Baptist churches had been established. Later, through the World Mission Crusade, a considerable endowment was made possible for these purposes, which, beginning in 1947, assisted the students and indirectly the colleges. These funds were further augmented from the CHEC campaign. By 1962, for instance, the total number of students aided was 190, with individual grants ranging from $100 to $1,000. That year 1,040 high school seniors entered the competition. As changing cultural needs and patterns appeared, adjustments were made in the program. By the 1970s the need for assistance by those in minority groups had far outstripped other calls; so the decision was made to emphasize aid to the culturally disadvantaged. With endowment funds of about $1,500,000 bringing in an income of over $100,000 a year, some truly helpful contributions could be made. Currently (1973), about 40 percent of this goes directly to American Baptist related colleges for support of their scholarship programs to minority group students; another 7½ percent goes to assist pastors in their continuing education; and about 10 percent is used for grants to new seminary students. The newer programs of aid are being given increasing support as old ones are phased out.

In addition to these direct financial aids, ABC's Board of Educational Ministries through its Public Relations Services has contributed substantially to the schools, colleges, and seminaries. In terms of total funds involved, this feature far outdistanced all other means. Begun under Louis Robey and continued under Paul Carter and then under Lester Garner, the plan was, essentially, one of fund-raising counsel. Public Relations Services would review the fiscal needs and projects of related schools and colleges, consult with them, and suggest strategies. While the main responsibility of the work would rest upon the shoulders of the local staff, or professional fund-raisers if such were engaged, the American Baptist Public Relations people would be in constant contact. This position of watchful and impartial advocacy enabled the denomination to multiply its direct support, that is, the budget of the Public Relations Division, manyfold. For instance, in 1964, the Division was able to help Colgate Rochester Divinity School reach it challenge goal of $675,000.

At the same time as the Division was assisting educational organizations directly, it was also promoting the use by local churches of the Institutional Support Program. Through the cooperation of the Convention at large, churches were encouraged to place an amount in their annual budgets for designated support to one or more American Baptist educational institutions, including schools, colleges, and seminaries. Thus, a total of $1,209,779 was contributed to the Institutional Support Program in 1966. Had this money come from invested funds, the capital amount would have had to exceed $25 million to provide a comparable income.

CAMPUS CHRISTIAN LIFE

In June, 1912, Newton C. Fetter became the Baptist university pastor at the University of Michigan. The following year, the fledgling Board of Education made its first appropriation to the budget for student work at Ann Arbor, Michigan. For the next forty years, except for one brief period, Dr. Fetter remained in one capacity or another with the Board. He retired as executive director of the Division of Secondary and Higher Education for the Board of Education and Publication in 1952. During those years much happened to Baptists and their place on the college campus.

For one thing, numerous institutions, once denominationally oriented, became independent. At the same time, state colleges and universities began to accelerate rapidly, offering low tuition and an astounding variety in curriculum at the taxpayer's expense. No longer did Baptist youth attend just Baptist schools; they went everywhere. In 1952, it was reported that some 42,000 Baptist students were attending non-Baptist colleges or universities.

To meet the spiritual needs of these students, several schemes were devised. One was to engage as campus ministers qualified persons with a solid academic background, religious insight, and a gift of working with older youth. Their congregations would be the Baptist students and any interested friends. The Baptist student center might be located in a nearby Baptist church, but more likely elsewhere. The activities would run the gamut from formal worship services to group socials, from Bible classes to political debates. There would be no regular membership; there would be lists of those concerned. Some of the most fruitful work was done in the campus pastor's office as he dealt personally with students and their problems. Sometimes there would be service projects to challenge the youth. Other times there would be student conferences in which to participate. By 1953, it could be reported that there were more than fifty such campus ministers at work among American Baptist students.

In addition, there were over three hundred pastors of Baptist churches in college communities who also took as part of their calling the shepherding of Baptist students. In these cases, the involvement and program might vary even more than where the ministry was campus oriented. In some cases the church found almost as much value in the relationship as did the students.

A marked change in direction for the campus ministry was taken in 1968 when the Board, on recommendation of its staff, entered its Department of Campus Christian Life into an ecumenical ministry known as the United Ministries in Higher Education (UMHE). Ten denominations agreed to pool their efforts and to work as one body on behalf of all. Several factors contributed to that decision, including rising student enrollments, diminishing financial support, declining denominational consciousness on the part of students, and the growing spirit of ecumenism. Resulting from this move came the addition of staff resource personnel with a wide background of expertise for the expansion of national programs in special areas, such as medical education, and the Black campus ministry. About 10 percent of the local ministries remained almost totally Baptist in their emphasis, with the others having varying degrees of cooperation all the way to a completely unified ministry in higher education. A similar pattern prevailed at the state and regional level with some states operating in the context of UMHE while others continued on a strictly denominational basis. In Baptist polity, this was completely appropriate. The effect, however, on the integrity of the various denominations as they look to the future remains, at this writing, unclear, especially with the concurrently growing strength of such nondenominational groups of a strictly evangelical nature as Campus Crusade and Inter-Varsity Fellowship.

BLACK COLLEGES IN THE SOUTH

The concerns of Baptists in the North for educational opportunities for freedom in the South following the Civil War have been noted. This interest and support continued over the years in varying degrees. Most of the colleges begun by the Baptists continued on a struggling basis and contributed greatly to the nation and the denomination through the efforts of their educated alumni. In 1971 there were six predominantly Black schools related to the American Baptist Board of Education and Publication, all fully accredited: Benedict, Columbia, South Carolina; Bishop, Dallas, Texas; Florida Memorial, Miami, Florida; Morehouse, Atlanta, Georgia; Shaw, Raleigh, North Carolina; and Virginia Union, Richmond, Virginia.

Ministerial education has been more slowly developed. It was reported in 1946 that "the few studies available indicate that 90 percent or more of the ministers of the 40,000 Negro Baptist churches in this country have only the scantiest elementary school education." This was a clear call to do something, and some of the colleges responded. For instance, Virginia Union developed its School of Theology, and Morehouse College opened a School of Religion. The latter became the Baptist unit in the Interdenominational Theological Center in Atlanta and gave significant leadership to the establishment of the first theological education cluster in America. Of even greater implication for American Baptists was the opening of many previously White seminaries to Black students. Thus Martin Luther King, Jr., was an alumnus of Crozer; Joseph H. Jackson, of the National Baptist Convention, Incorporated, and Gardner Taylor, of the Progressive National Baptist Convention, were graduates of Colgate Rochester. William T. McKee, appointed in 1973 as Associate General Secretary for Educational Ministries of the American Baptist Churches in the U.S.A., is also a Black graduate of Colgate Rochester.

It was of marked importance that the denomination's capital funds campaign scheduled for the mid-1970s took for its major goal the raising of substantial money for the strengthening of the Black Baptist colleges in the South. This was a cooperative effort of the

Progressive National Baptist and the American Baptist churches. Such concern by the sponsoring bodies was expected to elicit support from some of the major foundations, perhaps comparable to the Ford Foundation grants in 1969 of $1,212,000 to Shaw, and $365,000 to Benedict.

As with other colleges maintaining a relationship to the denomination, one of the strongest means of support has not been financial but advisory. Thus, the Division of Christian Higher Education has been helpful in the relocation of Florida Memorial to Miami and of Bishop College to Dallas. The upgrading of curricula and the conduct of administration have also been areas where American Baptist Churches' counsel has been helpful.

Bishop College, Dallas, Texas

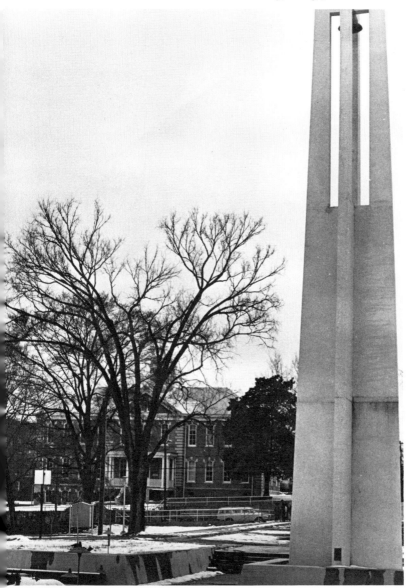

173

Valley F
Office Buil

10. New Dimensions *of Witness in the Churc*

Response to Changing Needs and Patterns in Church Education

It took no prophetic insight, no academic investigation, no computerized survey to conclude that the perils and problems of the educational program of the local church which had become apparent in the 1930s had not been solved by mid-century. Valiant attempts had been made, but few achievements could be reported. With a growing sophistication in society, a rising level of education, a shrinking of world distances, the budding of countercultures which would flower in the sixties and seventies, and a skyrocketing series of scientific achievements, it was not an easy time for the Christian church.

To meet the challenges offered by these conditions, the Board determined upon several strategies. It would develop new methods of encouragement for stabilizing and enlarging the educational work of the local church, and it would revise, continue, or develop materials which should prove useful in this task.

NEW PROGRAMS

In the spring of 1953, Dr. Kenneth L. Cober assumed the leadership of the Division of Education in Home, Church, and Community. The title was ponderous, but it was an accurate description of the position. Acting with vigor and with understanding of the needs, the new director soon was deeply involved in preparing plans to counteract the ennui which was afflicting much of the church school life. The result was a national program to redeem "the Sunday church school from its mediocrity." It was called the Year of Baptist Achievement, or YBA.

The YBA was founded on eight principles:

1. The New Testament exalts the ministry of Christian teaching.
2. Religion must be taught by the church or it will not be taught.
3. The Sunday church school is the church's chief agency for teaching religion.
4. Half of the children and youth of America are unreached by any religious teaching—Protestant, Catholic, or Jewish.
5. Increasing evidence of juvenile delinquency is a challenge to our Sunday church schools.
6. The Sunday church school is the church's chief evangelistic agency.
7. The Sunday church school faces its greatest opportunity in years. [This was based on the fact of a postwar rising birthrate statement.]
8. With a concerted and cooperative effort every Sunday church school can do its job better.

To put these ideas into motion, a nationwide team of Christian educators was organized, and workbooks containing details and directions were prepared. Much of the responsibility fell upon clusters of churches which often coincided with associational groups. Training conferences were held. Form letters for use by local and district leaders were prepared, and numerous rallies and gatherings were used to generate interest and enthusiasm. Job descriptions for each local church pastor and Sunday school divisional officer were carefully prepared.

YBA was a massive effort of American Baptist churches to lift themselves by their own educational bootstraps. Some positive results were noted. Many churches, 3,602 to be exact, participated, including most of the active churches in the American Baptist Convention. On an average, these churches reported an 8 percent increase in Sunday church school enrollment and a 10 percent increase in attendance. They also reported an average increase of 2 newly organized classes per church. A total of 240,688 calls were made in the homes of prospects. Many churches organized boards of Christian education for the first time, and nearly 20,000 leadership education credits were issued. It seems safe to say that this intensive program did more than any other single factor to guide American Baptist Sunday schools in the two decades following its introduction.

AREA DIRECTORS

From the very beginning, the Publication Society has been a missionary organization. In the earliest years its agents went everywhere organizing Sunday schools, distributing Christian literature, and giving encouragement to local pastors and leaders. This work of the Society and of its successor, the Board, never ceased, but the approach varied with times and occasions. By the beginning of the second century of endeavor, the Society was helping to place a Christian education staff person on the roster of every state convention and city society related to the American Baptist Convention. The major responsibility for administration of this large staff fell upon the director of the Division of Christian Education (later known as the Division of Church Education). This was usually a cooperative effort supported jointly by the region, state, or city and the Board, with the direct administrative responsibility being carried by the local area. The investment in time and talent of this contribution by the national board of the denomination cannot be measured, but the financial commitment can. This varied in the period 1950–1972 from $65,000 to $100,000. The higher figure was reached in 1964 and the lower in 1972. The list of area directors has included many persons who have moved on to other significant areas of service in the denomination, headed perhaps by Edwin H. Tuller, onetime director in Connecticut who served as general secretary of ABC from 1950 to 1970.

Although accountability was always to the local administrative area, the nature of the situation—joint appointment, mutual financial support, and professional counsel—has, in a sense given the Board of Educational Ministries a representative on the staff of every region, state, and city area of the American Baptist Churches, a feature not shared by either the National or International Ministries' boards. Such a service has proved to be a stabilizing and unifying influence in a denomination founded on the autonomy of the local church and the competency of the individual believer.

CHRISTIAN PUBLICATIONS

The Publication Society began, as we have seen, as an agency to produce Christian literature. It never has lost that commitment. As the demand for highly specialized materials rose to satisfy the requirements of a more sophisticated age, the Society's writers, editors, artists, and printers strove to meet the need. Baptist churches were faithfully supplied over the years with carefully designed materials for the full program of Christian education at prices which the vast majority could afford to pay.

In 1945, for instance, it could be reported that the Society was publishing in the children's division 38 different units of the Judson Keystone Graded materials, 6 units of the International Uniform Lessons, 2 story papers, plus other regular features in *Baptist Leader*. In the youth division there were 16 units of the Keystone Graded materials being published, 4 units of the Uniform Lessons, 2 Sunday evening youth fellowship magazines, 2 story papers, and materials in *Baptist Leader*. The adults were not given as wide a choice, but nevertheless there were 4 units of Uniform Lessons, extensive material in *Baptist Leader, Home* magazine, and other publications.

To head the post of this important work as editor-in-chief in 1947 came Dr. Benjamin P. Browne, a man remarkably suited to the task. Born and educated in New England, he had served as pastor, as promotion director for Massachusetts, as executive secretary for the Baptist convention in Pennsylvania, and in various college and seminary trusteeships. He was a talented author and preacher, warmly and openly evangelical in his theological position. In his first full report to the constituency he made his position crystal clear:

> While our materials have always been definitely pointed to the winning of boys and girls to Christ and his Kingdom, evangelism will be given an even larger place in our materials, as will the recognition that life situations must be viewed in the light the Word of God throws upon them. Our materials will remain true to our historic Baptist faith and principles—infused with the missionary message and passion, world-envisioned with the challenge of Christ to every realm of life. He must indeed become the "Lord of all worlds" known to man.

Dr. Browne knew where he wanted to go, but with a pluralistic Convention of churches making a wide variety of demands and with a schedule calling for 117 different publications a year, the achievement was not easy. Under his direction the staff launched the development of a new curriculum. The new Judson Graded Series was begun in 1947 and took several years to complete. By 1955, Browne could write that "this new Judson curriculum for American Baptist churches is surpassing expectations, and we are happy to learn that American Baptist teaching materials for our Sunday church schools are now enjoying a wider use than at any time in the last twenty-five years."

Dr. Browne was succeeded in the early 1960s by Dr. Glenn Asquith, an equally well-known author, pastor, and administrator. And what do we find Glenn Asquith doing? Accepting the current curriculum? Not at all! It was apparent that more work needed to be done at this point in time and a specialist in curriculum research, Dr. Richard Gladden, was engaged for this purpose. Currently, several other religious groups were also busy at a similar endeavor; so it became feasible to do the project on a cooperative basis. Eventually sixteen denominations were involved in what came to be known as the Cooperative Curriculum Project. American Baptists were represented at one time or another by twenty-four staff members not only from the Board of Education and Publication but also from other agencies of the denomination. This relationship reflected the concern that the curriculum design should be comprehensive and churchwide. The denominations participating in the project included: Advent Christian Church, African Methodist Episcopal Church, American Baptist Convention, Disciples of Christ, Church of the Brethren, Church of God, Church of the Nazarene, Cumberland Presbyterian Church, Evangelical United Brethren Church, Mennonite Church, Methodist Church, Presbyterian Church in Canada, Presbyterian Church in the U.S., Protestant Episcopal Church, Southern Baptist Convention, and the United Church of Canada.

The product of this far-ranging research project was a treatment of biblical theology, educational methodology, and human growth and developmental characteristics in such a way as to provide basic resources for the several denominational curriculum planners. The Curriculum Plan that resulted was essentially a document to be used as a resource in the educational ministry of Protestant churches. It was a tool to assist in the process of constructing specific curriculum plans or designs for denominations.

Some of the groups took this basic data and produced their own denominational materials. Others entered into cooperative ventures. Among the latter initally were the American Baptist Convention, the Disciples of Christ, the Church of the Brethren, the Church of God (Anderson, Indiana), and some representatives of the All-Canada Baptist Publishing Committee. Subsequently, the Church of God, with the help of their own editors and writers, published a separate curriculum.

Dr. Asquith provided leadership in the early stages of the American Baptist cooperative venture but resigned before final publication. He and Dr. Kenneth Cober were succeeded by Grant W. Hanson, a professional Christian educator from California, upon the merger of the two divisions which Asquith and Cober had headed.

The Christian Faith and Work Plan, which was the American Baptist version, was an ambitious and expensive endeavor. American Baptists, for instance, invested more than one million dollars in developmental costs but saved approximately half a million over and above this amount by sharing the work with other denominations. The Faith and Work Graded Series for the church school, which resulted from this project, was introduced to American Baptist churches in the fall of 1969. A prodigious amount of time, effort, and talent had gone into it. Initially the churches viewed the new curriculum with interest, and many invested in the material, but some found it not to their liking. The pluralism of the Convention which had been so apparent a generation before was still present. Indeed, the variations had even multiplied although, providentially, the rancor had not.

The awareness of the need for a bold new strategy was growing. The recognition of the wide diversity of American Baptists received increased attention. It became obvious that the self-determined needs of all the churches were not being met. Churches insisted that they knew best what they required with respect to teaching resources. In direct response to the needs of the churches the Board adopted two strategies designed to serve these curriculum concerns.

The first strategy was to provide an additional curriculum option to the two existing series. The publication rights to the graded series developed by the Church of God (Anderson, Indiana) from the Cooperative Project were purchased. Baptist editors turned to the task of reworking the material for American Baptist use. The new materials were to be known as the Bible and Life Graded Series and would stress the approach to life issues from the biblical perspective. The second strategy was the introduction of the concept of Individual Curriculum Planning. This provided the tools which allowed each church to survey its educational needs and decide in its own way which of the three series of curriculum materials published by the Board of Educational Ministries would be best suited to its needs.

The decision would be made by those most deeply involved in the teaching ministry of the individual church.

The churches were asked to make their selections from three options: the Uniform Bible Series, the Bible and Life Graded Series, and the Faith and Work Graded Series. The churches responded most favorably to this new approach. By the close of 1972, there were probably about six hundred churches using the Bible and Life Graded Series, perhaps twice as many following the Uniform Bible Series and approximately three times as many using the Faith and Work Graded Series. In addition, numerous churches used various other curriculum materials from other Baptist publishers or from independent commercial firms. There were also churches with talented leadership that wrote and used their own materials. Probably at no time in the history of American Baptists had there been such diversity in the employment of Christian educational materials.

Minority groups were also a concern. The Board of Educational Ministries responded to the pleas of the churches of the Hispanic caucus by developing *Fe y Vida,* a Spanish-language quarterly for youth and adults. Although no special publications were developed for Black churches, Black editors and artists participated in development of most materials, and all texts reflected a concern for the Black experience.

In addition to its publications, the Division of Church Education provided leadership for the churches in the development of skills and understandings through a diversity of field programs, including family life education, Green Lake laboratory schools, a National Leader Corps, a variety of national and regional training events, experimentation with new models of Christian education, and many other activities.

PUBLISHING AND BUSINESS

Undergirding and supporting this ministry in Christian education and publications was the Division of Publishing and Business. The executive director of the Division, who came to the office in 1967, was Peter A. Jensh. Moving directly from the business world of a large insurance company in New England, he brought the knowledge and craftsmanship so necessary to an operational officer. The times were not propitious for publishers of religious literature. In 1970, for instance, the Methodist Publishing House reported a net loss of over one and one-third million dollars. Christian book concerns in Great

Britain were described as "facing a financial crisis." The United Presbyterian Church, U.S.A., found it necessary in 1971 to approve a budget for its Board of Christian Education that was two-thirds of a million dollars below the previous year. In secular journalism some old established magazines, such as *Life, Look,* and *The Saturday Evening Post,* had closed or were about to close due to constantly rising costs of manufacturing and circulation.

The American Baptist Board of Education and Publication was not immune to the economic and social milieu. A steadily declining church school enrollment only compounded the situation. Sunday school enrollment among American Baptists, which had ranged around the million mark for decades, had dropped to 670,741 by 1968. From 1961 to 1969 the Board had operated on a deficit basis which ultimately accumulated to $1,333,309. To this serious problem Mr. Jensh and a team consisting of Paul V. Moore, treasurer, and Donald C. Burkholder, controller, addressed itself.

The year 1970 revealed a much better financial picture for the Board than had been noted for some time. Through exacting economies, the addition of modern manufacturing equipment and methods, the reduction of nonessential employees, the gaining of most of the denomination's printing business (much of which had been sent by other agencies to outside printers), and the vigorous pursuit of general printing services, the operations of the Board were rebalanced, with a modest surplus which was used to begin repayment of some of the indebtedness from prior years.

In that year, 1970, the total income from sales and services came to nearly $5.4 million. The cost to develop, manufacture, distribute, and service the various publications of the Board totaled $5.8 million. The other activities of the Board added nearly one million dollars bringing the magnitude of the operation to $6.7 million. Of this, $1,027,214 came from the churches through their gifts to the Basic Mission Budget and other designations, while invested funds of the Board brought in roughly $300,000. Samuel Cornelius, who had helped spark the idea of a Baptist publishing business 150 years earlier by carrying tracts around in his hat, would have been astounded.

A part of the happening was the vigorous development of Judson Press. Under this name, the Publication Society many years before had entered the book-producing field. In 1970, thirty-eight books were published. With 5,000 copies normally printed as a first edition, it may be noted that three of the books went into second printings before the end of the year. They were: *Make Mine Coffee, Team Building in Church Groups,* and *The Black Vanguard.* Indicating the international scope of Judson Press, thirteen of the books on the 1970 list were American editions of overseas publications, ten from Great Britain, two from Japan, and one from France. At the same time, Judson books from America were issued by publishers in Great Britain, France, Japan, Germany, and Italy. The range of titles in 1970 ran the gamut of Baptist interest from *Mr. Bear Goes to Sea* for children to a substantial volume by Robert B. Laurin, *Contemporary Old Testament Theologians.*

Producing this vast array of materials—Sunday school curriculum series, religious books, denominational materials, and outside publications—there is a modern printing plant, completed with the general headquarters building at Valley Forge in 1962. Here one finds not only the usual flatbed presses, but also a large web offset press with built-in folding equipment which has a production rate more than ten times faster than the traditional combination of flatbed press and separate folder. Type is set on modern computer-controlled phototypesetting equipment. Computer-prepared labels are affixed by a fully automated mailing machine. Ninety people manufacture and distribute the millions of pieces of curriculum resources, books, and magazines to the four retail stores maintained by the Board, to other religious bookstores across the nation, and to thousands of local churches and individual purchasers.

EXECUTIVE DIRECTION

As chief of this vast complex of educational ministries of American Baptists came Dr. Harold W. Richardson in 1964 following the retirement of Dr. Richard Hoiland. He brought with him the administrative talents he had demonstrated for many years as president of Franklin College in Indiana.He brought also with him the insights of sensitivities gained in earlier years as a pastor. Also, he brought with him the skills and talents of a trained psychologist—this was his postgraduate specialty. As a result, the inner tensions which so often disturb and hinder the efficient operation of an agency as large and complex as the Board of Educational Ministries were often nonexistent. Quiet and calm efficiency prevailed in the Board of Education and Publication under Harold Richardson.

Following Dr. Richardson's retirement in 1973, came Dr. William McKee to the post of Associate General Secretary for Educational

Richard Hoiland

Harold W. Richardson

William T. McKee

Ministries of the American Baptist Churches. Prior to this responsibility, Dr. McKee had served for nearly ten years with the Ministers and Missionaries Benefit Board in various capacities, finally as associate director. A native of Brooklyn, New York, he had grown up in the Berean Baptist Church there and had received his education in Brooklyn College and New York University. Graduate study took him to Colgate Rochester Divinity School, Dillard University in New Orleans, and Harvard Business School. He was the first Black person to head a major program board for American Baptists.

ADDED MINISTRIES

In the extensive reorganization of the American Baptist household made in Denver, 1972, through the Study Commission on Denominational Structure (SCODS), there were added other departments to the Board of Education and Publication. These organizations to be administratively related were the American Baptist Historical Society, American Baptist Men, American Baptist Women, and the Division of Communication. At this time the Board's name was changed to the Board of Educational Ministries.

The American Baptist Historical Society had been founded by the Publication Society at a special meeting held May 5, 1853, in the Spruce Street Church, Philadelphia. Later, it had been separated from the parent body and had become the chief repository for Baptist records and documents with library facilities on the premises of the Colgate Rochester/Bexley Hall/Crozer Divinity School. In the publishing field, the Society could report in 1971 the issuance of Volume 16 of its exhaustive and detailed *Baptist Bibliography.* This carries a listing of Baptist authors and their works through Merrimac—Nevins. The demand for this remarkably complete record of Baptist, and anti-Baptist, writings was so substantial that Volume 7 had to be reprinted in 1971 and Volume 8 in 1972. The journal of Baptist history and theology, *Foundations,* is also a responsibility of the Historical Society and repeated requests for back issues have led to the decision to produce the back file on microfilm.

American Baptist Men, begun in 1912 by the Publication Society as its Department of Social Service and Baptist Brotherhood but long an autonomous agency within the American Baptist Convention, was also added administratively to the Board of Educational Ministries. The Men had long been active in the support of Green Lake and in the efforts to involve laymen more deeply in the life of the local church.

American Baptist Women began in 1914 as a committee allied with the Woman's American Baptist Foreign Mission Society and its counterpart in the Woman's American Baptist Home Mission Society. It became the National Committee on Women's Work, then the National Council of American Baptist Women, and in 1965 the American Baptist Women. As its origin indicates, the division was always highly motivated in the direction of mission support. Its promotion and supervision of the gathering and distribution of White Cross materials so important to medical and relief work at the Baptist stations around the world have been legendary. Its sponsorship of the Love Gift offering each year has also been notable for achievement. In 1970, for example, this offering amounted to $678,599, not an inconsiderable amount of the denomination's whole mission budget. In recent years a new dimension has been added to the group's interest. This was a campaign for increased opportunities for women on the professional level and for the development of women's lay leadership in the churches. Since the denomination is reliably reported to consist of 63 percent women, the potential is obviously very great.

The Division of Communication, long related directly to the Convention, was in 1972 placed administratively under the Board of Educational Ministries. The move was a logical one since it was this department that had responsibility for the publication of *The American Baptist* magazine and *Input,* a weekly newsletter issued to augment the magazine. With a paid circulation of approximately 200,000 *The American Baptist* reaches the majority of concerned church members in the ABC. The Division also prepared and published the *American Baptist News Service* material, a mimeographed weekly resumé of approximately eight pages of Baptist and other religious news intended especially for use by the religious and secular press. The electronic media were also served by the Division through the production of cassette tapes, radio programs, and TV shows. All of these efforts were modern applications of the old tract society mission, the multiplying of the witness, the dissemination of "evangelical truth," and the inculcation of "sound morals." To the printing press have been added the facilities of the electronic media to the end that God might be known in Jesus Christ.

A printing press in the old Philadelphia printing plant

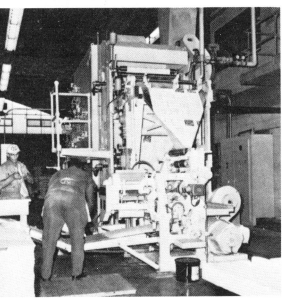

High speed web offset press in the Valley Forge plant

Computerized typesetting in the Valley Forge plant

187

Appendix
Members of the
Board of Managers
since 1924

Prepared by Madelene L. Andrews

Members of the A.B.P.S. Board for its first century following its founding have been listed in Daniel Gurden Stevens, *The First Hundred Years of The American Baptist Publication Society* (Philadelphia: A.B.P.S., 1924) and Lemuel Call Barnes, *et al.,* *Pioneers of Light* (Philadelphia: A.B.P.S., 1924). The purpose of the following listing is merely to supplement that earlier directory, providing the names of all members of the educational, publication, or combined boards since 1924; and members of the educational board prior to that time, in a separate list.

BOARD OF EDUCATION OF THE NORTHERN BAPTIST CONVENTION
(Not continuing beyond 1924)

Arnett, Trevor, 1915–1921
Ayer, Mrs. F. W., 1921–1924

Broadway, Rev. A. L., 1919–1923
Brock, C. R., 1921–1924
Brougher, Rev. J. Whitcomb, Sr., 1912–1916

Chandler, C. Q., 1912–1915
Clark, Sidney, 1911–1914
Colgate, Sidney, 1915–1918
Cope, Prof. H. F., 1919–1921

Deeds, E. A., 1916–1918

Ewart, A. W., 1912–1914

Farmer, Mrs. W. H., 1919–1922
Faunce, W. H. P., 1911–1915

Fosdick, Rev. Henry E., 1912–1913
Foster, Rev. A. K., 1912–1920
Franklin, John E., 1912–1915

Johnson, Grafton, 1922–1923

Marsh, Charles A., 1913–1921

Price, Prof. I. M., 1919–1920
Price, Pres. S. E., 1915–1924

Robins, Prof. H. B., 1919–1923

Strong, Pres. Frank, 1911–1917

Townson, A. J., 1912–1914
Tustin, Hon. Ernest L., 1912–1916

Woelfkin, Rev. Cornelius, 1912–1915

BOARD MEMBERS SINCE 1924

Service dates are inclusive, including the "combined boards."

A— member served only on the American Baptist Publication Society Board of Managers
B— member served only on the Board of Education of the Northern Baptist Convention
C—   "   "   on both boards
D—   "   "   on combined boards, the Board of Education and Publication of the Northern Baptist Convention and after 1950 of the American Baptist Convention, and after 1973 of the Board of Educational Ministries of the American Baptist Churches in the U.S.A.

D	Adams, Prof. W. W.,	1944–1950	D	Bartlett, Rev. Gene E.,	1948–1957
D	Anderson, David,	1967–1970	D	Barton, Amos B.,	1962–1967
B	Anderson, Pres. E. J.,	1940–1943	B-C	Beaven, Pres. Albert W.,	1928–1945
A-C	Arbuckle, Charles N., D.D.,	1922–1945	B	Behan, Pres. W. P.,	1940–1943
D	Armacost, Pres. George A.,	1946–1952	D	Belli, Rev. William R.,	1969–
D	Armacost, Pres. Peter,	1971–	D	Bettison, Morse,	1948–1951
D	Armstrong, Rev. Homer J.,	1951–1954	D	Beynon, Mrs. Lee J., Jr.,	1959–1968
			B	Bigelow, Prof. Bruce M.,	1937–1943
			C	Bigelow, Rev. Gordon,	1941–1946
D	Bailey, Henry Turner,	1923–1931	D	Bishop, Rev. Russell H.,	1954–1964
A	Bainbridge, Harry,	1918–1932	D	Blake, Prof. I. G.,	1947–1950
A	Baker, F. Raymond,	1935–1943	D	Bloomquist, Rev. Earl, Sr.,	1954–1963
D	Ballenger, Rev. M. C.,	1971–	A	Bluemle, Lewis W.,	1933–1941
D	Banes, Fred W., Ph.D.,	1961–1972	D	Boddie, Dr. Charles E.,	1947–1956
B	Barbour, Pres. Clarence A.,	1911–1937	D	Bonell, Rev. H. C.,	1948–1954
D	Barbosa, David,	1972–	D	Boutwell, Dr. A. H.,	1960–1963

D	Brooks, Rev. Henry C.,	1971–
D	Brougher, Rev. J. W., Jr.,	1940–1947
D	Brown, Miss Alberta F.,	1964–1967
D	Brown, Rev. Carl H., Th.D	1968–
B	Brown, Prof. J. S.,	1915–1935
C-D	Brown, Dr. Kenneth I.,	1941–1961
D	Bryant, Elliott D.,	1953–1956
D	Buchanan, Mrs. E. W.,	1957–1966
B	Burton, Pres. Ernest DeW.,	1911–1925
B	Burton, Miss Margaret E.,	1926–1944
B	Campbell, Leroy,	1940–1943
D	Campbell, Robert C., Th.D.,	1957–1960
		and 1965–1972
D	Camper, Glenn E.,	1965–1970
D	Carder, Rev. E. C.,	1936–1952
D	Caverly, E. R.,	1941–1948
C-D	Charters, W. W., Ph.D.,	1921–1952
	(did not serve 1924–1926, or	
	for 1948–1949)	
D	Chastain, Rev. Theron M.,	1951–1954
D	Clark, Mrs. Adrian,	1964–1968
D	Clark, Rev. William P.,	1970–
A	Clegg, John, W.,	1920–1926
A	Cole, Henry E.,	1918–1941
B	Coleman, Mrs. G. W.,	1928–1932
D	Colmer, Earl B.,	1922–1950
B	Condon, Randall J.,	1928–1931
B	Cortner, George P.,	1932–1937
D	Craig, Rev. Robert T.,	1946–1951
B	Crandall, Mrs. L. A.,	1919–1928
A	Cressman, Harvey E.,	1931–1934
B	Curry, Rev. E. R.,	1911–1931
D	Curry, Frank W.,	1960–1969
B	Cutten, Pres. George G.,	1931–1945
D	Daane, Prof. A. H.,	1960–1963
D	Dahlberg, Rev. Edwin T.,	1938–1948
A	Dakin, Rev. E. Leroy,	1922–1927
D	Dana, Pres. H. E.,	1944–1946
D	Dannenhauer, Kenneth,	1944–1947
D	Davison, Rev. A. C.,	1949–1952
D	Day, Rev. Duane L.,	1952–1955
B	Deems, Rev. Charles E.,	1935–1941
D	Deibler, Samuel E., Jr.,	1971–
D	Dice, Rev. Merris,	1968–1970
D	Didier, Rev. James,	1970–
D	Dodge, Mrs. F. A.,	1960–1964
D	Dold, Miss Diane Doane,	1953–1954
D	Dollar, Miss Carrie,	1944–1946
D	Dowdy, Rev. R.,	1961–1968
		and 1969–1972
D	Durden, Rev. Charles,	1946–1949

D	Eckman, Miss Lynne,	1961–1964
A	Elliott, Rev. William A.,	1934–1943
B	Elliff, Prof. J. D.,	1935–1941
D	Erickson, Rev. Walfred,	1957–1966
D	Eubank, Mrs. Earle,	1941–1952
D	Eulette, Mrs. Clayton D.,	1922–1954
B	Evans, Rev. D. J.,	1920–1932
D	Fagerburg, Rev. Frank B.,	1937–1943
D	Fenton, Jerry,	1957–1961
D	Fewster, Lowell,	1960–1962
D	Fields, Wayne D.,	1962–1967
A	Fisher, Charles E.,	1932–1932
B	Foster, Mrs. Katherine C.,	1933–1942
D	Foster, R. Lee, M.D.,	1956–1965
D	Fowler, Rev. Fenwick T.,	1961–1964
D	Fox, Paul Drewry,	1960–
D	Fraser, Rev. John F.,	1957–1958
D	Frazee, Rev. Harold B.,	1964–1969
D	Fredrikson, Rev. Roger L.,	1945–1949
		and 1955–1960
	″	1961–1970
D	Freiert, Mrs. Jerry C.,	1954–1956
	(Barbara Jones)	
D	Fromm, H. Gordon,	1954–1957
D	Gates, Rev. Elbert E., Jr.,	1965–1973
D	Gerlitz, Rev. Eugene F.,	1958–1967
B	Gilkey, Rev. Charles W.,	1927–1933
B	Gillette, L. S.,	1912–1924
B	Goodchild, Rev. F. M.,	1921–1928
D	Goodman, Miss Vera,	1972–
B	Gosnell, A. J.,	1936–1942
D	Green, Howard,	1948–1953
D	Gregerson, Miss Lucile,	1967–
A	Griffith, J. P. Crozer, M.D.,	1912–1944
B	Hanley, Rev. Elijah A.,	1913–1940
D	Hanold, Miss Kathleen,	1963–1972
A	Harms, Rev. A. J.,	1935–1938
D	Hass, Rev. L. H. R.,	1961–1964
D	Hauseman, Rev. Francis K.,	1961–1970
D	Heaton, Rev. C. Adrian,	1956–1965
B	Heimsath, Mrs. C. H.,	1940–1943
D	Hermann, Miss Cay,	1947–1950
C	Herrick, Pres. Everett C.,	1933–1946
D	Hicks, Weimer K., LL.D.,	1963–
D	Hitch, Rev. Francis M.,	1967–
D	Hodson, Rev. E. Woody,	1939–1946
B	Hollingshead, Pres. B. S.,	1941–1944
D	Holstine, Garold D.,	1959–1967
D	Honts, Rev. Ernest L.,	1946–1952
B	Hopkins, Pres. E. M.,	1924–1928
A	Hoot, Wesley H.,	1929–1931
	″ ″ (Recording Sec.)	1930–1943

190

D	Hopper, H. Boardman,	1920–1960
B	Horr, Pres. George E.,	1911–1929
D	Houser, Mrs. A. P., Jr.,	1938–1947
D	Huber, Miss Evelyn,	1955–1960
D	Huchingson, Pres. J. E.,	1944–1950
B	Hunt, Pres. Emory W.,	1911–1938
D	Hunt, Rev. Horace H.,	1970–
D	Jackson, Rev. John H.,	1970–
A-C	Jackson, Rev. L. Earl,	1936–1946
D	Jenkins, Harry L., Esq.,	1922–1972
D	Johnson, Rev. Gove G.,	1921–1945
D	Johnson, Mrs. Major L.,	1952–1961
D	Johnson, Rev. R. Lewis,	1964–1966
D	Johnson, Robert L.,	1955–1965
D	Jones, Rev. E. Theodore,	1969–
D	Jones, Mrs. Idris W.,	1963–1966
D	Jones, Raymond D.,	1965–1968
D	Kelsey, Dr. George,	1956–1958
A	Kenney, Orrin P.,	1927–1936
D	Kierstead, Dr. G. B.,	1952–1961
D	Kleinsasser, Dennis,	1959–1962
D	Knudsen, Dr. Ralph E.,	1952–1961
D	Lance, Darrell,	1956–1957
B	Latourette, Prof. K. W.,	1920–1935
A	Lawson, Rev. A. G.,	1893–1895
		and 1919–1929
D	Lee, Rev. Allan,	1971–
D	Lee, Howard,	1967–1970
D	Lee, Mrs. Merritt R.,	1946–1955
B	Lent, Pres. Frederick,	1932–1942
D	Lichtenstein, David B.,	1954–1960
B	Lindsay, F. H.,	1927–1928
A	Lloyd, Rev. Joseph H.,	1937–1943
D	LoBello, Mrs. Leonard,	1955–1959
	(Joyce Parr)	
D	Logan, Rev. J. Paul,	1956–1965
D	Lopez, Rev. Noe R.,	1970–
D	Loughhead, Mrs. LaRue,	1966–
A-C	McAlpin, Rev. C. A.,	1942–1946
D	McClernon, Rev. Robert,	1961–1965
D	McDermott, Mrs. F. W.,	1956–1965
D	McDonald, Rev. Osgoode,	1937–1954
D	McLear, William Z.,	1940–1972
D	McDormand, Dr. Thomas B.,	1961–1967
A	MacFarlane, H. King,	1918–1940
B	MacIntosh, Prof. D. C.,	1937–1941
B	MacLeish, Mrs. Andrew,	1919–1938
B	Mann, Dean A. R.,	1929–1941
D	Marks, D. D.,	1949–1952

D	Martin, Andrew B.,	1967–1968
B	Mather, Kirtley F.,	1935–1937
D	Mason, Rev. Elliott, Sr.,	1969–
D	Maughan, Rev. Donald E.,	1970–
B-C	Merriam, Prof. Thornton,	1941–1946
D	Miller, James C.,	1958–1962
D	Miller, Pres. J. H.,	1941–1950
D	Mitchell, Mrs. Henry H.,	1959–1973
D	Mitchell, Richard W.,	1962–1965
D	Moe, Mrs. Lee A.,	1947–1956
B	Monroe, Prof. Paul,	1922–1933
D	Moor, Dr. George Caleb,	1942–1957
D	Morgan, Rev. Carl H.,	1950–1956
D	Morong, Dr. Carrol O.,	1950–1956
A	Morris, Rev. C. E.,	1941–1942
D	Nakagawa, Mr. Yosh,	1972–
D	Nelson, Rev. O. Dean,	1963–1971
D	Nelson, Harlon,	1965–1970
D	Nielsen, Helmar,	1956–1957
D	Norris, Mrs. Carter,	1947–1956
D	Palazzi, Miss Deborah,	1964–1968
D	Packer, Dr. Wilfred T.,	1956–1965
D	Palmer, Densley H., Ph.D.,	1966–1972
D	Palmquist, Theodore R.,	1965–1971
D	Parkinson, Rev. H. Lloyd,	1936–1954
D	Parsons, Rev. Spencer,	1944–1948
B	Pendleton, Pres. Ellen F.,	1923–1926
D	Pekrul, Rev. Melvin A.,	1965–
B	Philbrick, Mrs. H. S.,	1932–1941
D	Pierce, Richard H.,	1956–1960
A	Pierce, Rev. Robert F. Y.,	1912–1935
B	Pierson, Pres. R. A.,	1924–1927
D	Pixley, Rev. George V.,	1966–1969
		and 1970–
D	Plank, William H.,	1961–1969
B	Poteat, John,	1926–1930
D	Powell, Rev. Grady W.,	1966–
B	Price, Pres. M. B.,	1924–1936
D	Prince, Albert I.,	1953–1956
D	Prior, Rev. J. M.,	1941–1951
D	Proctor, Rev. Samuel D.,	1964–1965
D	Race, Norman B.,	1953–1960
D	Rae, Rev. W. Douglas,	1960–1968
A	Rannels, Rev. Charles H.,	1924–1936
D	Rasmussen, Robert T.,	1972–
A	Reese, B. E.,	1930–1931
D	Renshaw, Philip,	1966–1973
A	Rhoades, John D., Esq.,	1916–1937
D	Richardson, Rev. Harold W.,	1950–1959
D	Rider, Rev. Daniel G.,	1961–1969
B	Riley, Pres. Leonard W.,	1922–1940
D	Rivenburg, Dr. Romeyn H.,	1924–1954

191